Eliminate Negative Thinking

How to Overcome Negativity, Control Your Thoughts, And Stop Overthinking. Shift Your Focus into Positive Thinking, Self-Acceptance, And Radical Self Love

Derick Howell

Your Free Gift

This book includes a free bonus booklet. All information on how you can quickly secure your free gift can be found at the end of this book. It may only be available for a limited time.

TABLE OF CONTENTS

INTRODUCTION

Negative thinking is a very common problem that most people have encountered at some point in their lives. Although positive thinking is widely advocated by many health and wellness experts, getting yourself out of the rut of negative thoughts can be very challenging. Even if you are a person who analyzes their thoughts frequently, it can be difficult to tell the difference between negative thinking, and the everyday worries and anxieties that everyone deals with.

While it is normal to worry about issues such as divorce and financial problems, when these thoughts become too intrusive and unrelenting, they may wreak havoc not only on your personal life but also on your career and professional relationships.

It is for this reason that you need to understand what negative thinking is, how it manifests in your life and how you can overcome it. In doing so, you will be able to safeguard your mental health, become more resilient to change and be more capable of dealing with any challenges that come up in your personal and professional life.

So what is negative thinking and how do you determine which thoughts represent normal levels of concern and which are overly negative?

In general, negative thinking refers to a thought process in which one only sees the worst aspects of things, events, people and experiences. A negative thinker will always expect the worst possible outcome from every situation. Most people who engage in constant negative thinking also tend to reduce their expectations. They do this by considering only the worst possible scenarios in order to shield themselves from disappointment. Moreover, it is not uncommon for individuals who engage in negative thinking to suffer from low self-esteem and low self-confidence, since they are likely to focus on the things they consider inadequate about themselves.

Negative thinking may arise due to several factors. One of the most common causes of this type of thinking is depression. Most people experience a balanced mix of positive and negative thoughts throughout their day. Someone who has depression experiences a distorted view of the world, often through a filter of constant negative thinking. They may perceive themselves as a failure in life and unworthy of love or success. They may also view the world as inherently cruel and hostile. In addition to negative thinking, depression also affects the way individuals feel about themselves. People who are afflicted with this illness tend to feel very sad, despondent, fatigued and lethargic. This can compound the negative thinking and lead to even more serious health problems and sometimes, sadly, suicide. In most instances, people never realize that their negative thinking stems from depression. They may brush it off as simply being a normal part of who they are.

Another mental health condition that is closely associated with negative thinking is obsessive-compulsive disorder (OCD). Individuals who suffer from OCD typically experience unwanted, recurring thoughts and sensations which compel them to do certain things repeatedly, or in a very specific way. For instance, an OCD sufferer might feel the need to double-check their looks excessively, be fixated on organization, or repeat certain words or tasks repeatedly. Moreover, they might spend time "over cleaning" their clothes or washing their hands excessively due to an irrational fear of germs. This mental health condition is categorized as an anxiety disorder since the affected individuals perform these actions to lessen their anxiety. Due to this constant worry, people who have OCD tend to experience negative thinking more than those who don't. They may perceive themselves as being at risk of some impending danger if they do not satisfy these impulsive thoughts and needs. Even though most OCD sufferers tend to have an awareness that their obsessive thinking is not rooted in reality, they still find it difficult to control the behavior. Fortunately, this mental health condition, like many others, can be managed with the right help and support.

However, this does not mean that normal, healthy individuals are immune to the perils of negative thinking. In fact, there are plenty of reasons why even the most optimistic people find themselves in "negative thinking loops" at one point or another. Negative thoughts in most people arise out of fear of the future and anxiety about the prevailing circumstances in their lives. For instance, due to aging or time limitations, a person may worry about not achieving everything they had hoped to do in their lives. This might lead to feelings of anxiety, which if not confronted and dealt with, can affect one's mental and physical health. Some individuals may also feel anxious about past events, and how they have shaped their lives. This often leads to self-criticism, which may exacerbate negative thinking.

Regardless of where your negative thinking stems from, there is absolutely no reason why you should continue to wallow in these thoughts if they are affecting your life in negative ways. There are numerous techniques that can help you intercept your negative thoughts and manage them effectively when they arise.

I have been an anxiety coach for more than a decade. During this time, I have taught many individuals how to properly use these techniques to counter negative thoughts. I have also conducted numerous training workshops and seminars designed to help people overcome negative thinking loops which are holding them back from living their lives to the fullest.

There are many benefits to learning how to control negative thinking. Firstly, by countering your negative thoughts with positive thinking, you will be able to overcome mental illnesses such as depression and anxiety. You will also develop a more balanced perception of the world and yourself. In addition to this, you will be better equipped with the skills to cope with stressful life events and situations in a healthy way.

It is also no secret that anxiety and incessant worrying contributes to health problems such as hypertension and heart disease. By learning how to counter your negative thought loops, you can significantly reduce the risks of developing these health issues, which can be fatal if not managed effectively. So, by extension, getting yourself out of the rut of negative thoughts will help you increase your lifespan!

Unfortunately, overcoming negative thinking patterns is not as easy as most people think. As a person who has suffered from persistent negative thinking and anxiety, I can assure you that there are many challenges and obstacles that you will encounter along the way. This, however, should not cause you to lose hope! As long as you make a conscious resolve to end your negative thinking and are persistent about this goal, you will begin to enjoy remarkable results very soon. The tricks and techniques outlined in this book have helped not only myself but also thousands of other individuals throughout the world. I have no doubt, therefore, that they will work for you too, in your journey to overcome negative thinking.

So, if you are tired of negative thoughts getting in the way of your personal life, professional career or relationships, now is the time to nip this problem in the bud! I hope that you will find this book instructional and enjoyable, and that the wisdom contained herein will aid you in overcoming negative thinking, overthinking and anxiety, for good.

CHAPTER ONE:

Ineffective Ways to Stop Negative Thinking

If you struggle with negative thinking and anxiety, you are probably aware of how challenging it can be to change your mindset. Being stuck in negative thinking loops can feel like an internal struggle. On one hand, the psychological discomfort can be a strong motivator to pull yourself out of the rut, while on the other, you may not know exactly how to do so. This can leave you feeling very hopeless and frustrated.

Many people who engage in constant negative thinking resort to ineffective coping behaviors out of desperation (O'Brien, 2019a), which only makes the problem even more complex and much harder to solve.

In this chapter, we will discuss some of the ineffective ways of approaching negative thinking, and why you need to steer clear of them if you hope to get rid of your negative thoughts.

Ignoring the Negative Thoughts

Persistent negative thinking and overthinking can be very uncomfortable and disconcerting regardless of who you are. If you are constantly assailed by intrusive negative thoughts, you can feel very powerless and out of control. This is why most people resort to trying to ignore the negative thoughts in the hope that if they do not pay attention to them, they will magically go away. However, this doesn't always work out as expected. Negative thinking is usually a deep-seated internal problem that has taken a foothold in one's psyche. It is not something that can be easily wished away or ignored. While you might temporarily feel a sense of relief from not having to think about your negative thoughts, this relief is usually very short-lived and sooner or later, the negative thoughts may come bubbling to the surface once again.

Using Distractions and Diversions

Some people immerse themselves in their careers or hobbies in the hope that by distracting themselves from their negative thinking, it will somehow magically stop. People use expressions like "I'll just throw myself into my work," and "I'll just stay busy." However, this can be counterproductive, as it only shelves the problem rather than addressing it head-on and finding long-term solutions.

Indulging in Drugs and Alcohol

Constant negative thinking often leads to stress and anxiety, which can be very difficult to cope with. That is why many people resort to using products such as tobacco, marijuana, and alcohol in an effort to silence the negative thoughts in their head. However, while smoking and drinking alcohol can provide a temporary sense of relief, these are not very effective ways of dealing with negative thinking in the long-run. As a matter of fact, they can even lead to even more serious health problems such as dependency and addiction. It is worth noting that these methods of coping with negative thinking only offer temporary relief. While you might feel a sense of calm for a few hours, this soon dissipates once the effects of the drugs or alcohol wear off. Then you find yourself back in the cycle of negative thinking. In essence, drugs and alcohol only exacerbate the problem of negative thinking, and should, therefore, be avoided as a coping mechanism.

Bargaining with the Negative Thinking

It is not uncommon for some individuals to resort to bargaining with their negative thinking in an attempt to make it stop. They may be convinced that by trying to rationalize their thinking, they can pull themselves out of their negative thinking cycle. The problem with this kind of mentality is that it assumes that negative thinking is rooted in some kind of rationality. While this may be true in some cases, it does not apply in all instances. For example, the negative thoughts associated with depression may be the direct result of chemical imbalances in the brain.

Sleeping it Off

Getting adequate and quality sleep every night is beneficial in a number of ways. It helps in rejuvenating the body and the mind. It can also boost our thinking and memory.

However, despite its numerous benefits, overindulging in sleep as a means to counter negative thinking is not very effective. It only postpones the problem rather than solving it. This is not to say that you shouldn't use sleep as a temporary relief when you feel burnt out physically or mentally. In fact, sleeping can feel very refreshing, and be beneficial to your physical and mental well-being. However, you are advised not to use it as a crutch to avoid negative thinking patterns, as it may prevent you from dealing with the root of the problem. Remember, the goal is to find long-term solutions for your negative thinking problem. This is not something that sleeping will provide you with.

Resorting to these ineffective ways of dealing with negative thoughts has been shown to work only in the short term. Therefore, if you are trying to get rid of negative thinking permanently, it is absolutely crucial that you learn the proper techniques to approach the problem.

Summary

Now that you understand the ineffective ways of dealing with negative thinking, you are more likely to avoid them in the future. So, to recap this chapter, here are some of the big takeaways:

- Negative thinking is a problem that should never be ignored since this only postpones the solution and makes it more difficult to resolve.
- Using distractions to avoid your negative thoughts is counterproductive, and only delays and hinders you from coming up with long-term solutions.
- Drug and alcohol abuse only offers temporary relief from the discomfort of negative thoughts rather than providing permanent solutions.
- Do not try to argue with or rationalize your uncomfortable thoughts since negative thinking is an inherently irrational process.
- Sleeping does not effectively get rid of negative thinking. Rather, it shelves the problem, which means you will still have to deal with it later, when you wake up.

In the next chapter, we will cover ways in which you can clear your mind of negative thinking. The techniques and practices that will be discussed in the next chapter will be useful and handy to you. Pay close attention to them and see how they are applicable in your situation.

CHAPTER TWO:

Clear Your Mind of Negative Thinking

Negative thinking is a habit that can develop over time without the conscious awareness of an individual. If you allow negative thoughts to take hold in your mind, it will become very difficult to overcome them. However, this does not mean that you should immediately force negative thoughts out of your head the moment you become aware of them. As a matter of fact, the more you try to resist the thoughts, the stronger they become (Bloom, 2015). So what should you do in such a scenario?

Well, there are several practices and techniques you can employ to help you clear your mind of negative thoughts whenever they present themselves. Here are some of the ways in which you can counteract your negative thinking as soon as you become aware of it.

Change Your Body Language

Body posture is known to exert a significant influence on the way our minds work. For example, if you are slouching in an uncomfortable manner, you are likely to experience more negative thoughts than if you are at ease. In addition to this, poor body language can affect your self-image and confidence. This makes you more vulnerable to negative thinking and you may be prone to self-criticize. Therefore, it is vital to develop an awareness of your body language in order to get rid of persistent negative thinking more quickly.

Talk Them Through With Someone

There are times when negative thinking arises out of pent up emotions and feelings. Granted, most people find it uncomfortable to share their innermost feelings out of a fear of being judged by others. Other times it just seems like talking about your emotions with others amounts to burdening them with your problems. However, there are many benefits of sharing your uncomfortable emotions with people you trust. These include:

- You stand to gain a better perspective of your problems.
- You will be more likely to find a solution.
- You will be happy to know you are not alone.

Failing to share your uncomfortable feelings can seriously exacerbate the problem of negative thinking, and make you feel even more hopeless. Don't be alone with your negativity! Talking it out with someone you trust, on the other hand, can provide you with a sense of relief, and help dissipate your worries.

Spend a Minute Calming Your Mind

Negative thinking can become very overwhelming sometimes, causing you to feel anxious. Keeping your mind relaxed and at ease can be very challenging when you have a million thoughts racing around; therefore, it is very important to take some time to calm your mind. This will enable you to perceive things in a clear and unbiased way.

This requires taking a step back and letting the thoughts pass through your mind without offering any resistance or judgment. You can think of it as a kind of meditation. Once your thoughts have settled and your mind has calmed down sufficiently, you can then assess your thoughts from an objective point of view.

Change Your Perspective

Very often, we are plagued by negative thinking because of our poor perspective on the situations we encounter in life. Sometimes we find ourselves blaming the challenges we experience on a deficiency in ourselves. This can cause us to have a very poor self-image. However, all that is needed in some cases is simply a change of perspective. Instead of considering yourself as a failure when going through challenges, you can decide to think that you are no different from others who face day-to-day problems.

By changing your point of view whenever you feel assailed by negative thinking, you can develop self-confidence and clarity. Being able to look at your situation with an open mind will help you to identify the root cause of your negative thinking and assist you to troubleshoot it effectively.

Take Responsibility for Your Negative Thoughts

Many times when we are plagued with negative thoughts, it can be tempting to blame other people for the unpleasant situation which we may be facing. We might adopt a victim mentality or point a finger at other people as we try to avoid being accountable for the situation. This, however, is not a very effective way of dealing with uncomfortable or negative thoughts. While it might provide us with some temporary relief, it prevents us from considering the actual problem, thereby hindering us from finding long-lasting solutions. It is important to remember that even though you are not in control of everything that happens in your life, ultimately you are responsible for the choices you make and the outcomes which emerge as a result of those decisions. You should, therefore, learn to hold yourself accountable for any negative thoughts you may be experiencing. Take the initiative to seek out permanent solutions for them so that they do not interfere with your internal state of wellbeing.

Get Creative

While negative thoughts can be very unsettling psychologically due to the anxiety that they bring, they can also act as a catalyst for creativity. Whenever you feel overwhelmed by uncomfortable thoughts, you can use that opportunity to express yourself in creative ways.

You can channel your anxiety and frustration into creativity by writing, drawing, painting or even making music about it. Doing so allows you to find healthy outlets for your negative thoughts, thereby enabling you to purge them from your system. Furthermore, creating works of art also enables you to explore your emotions on a deeper level, thereby helping you to develop a better understanding of why you think the way you do.

Another fundamental benefit of being creative is that it helps you feel good about yourself. Channeling your mental discomfort into creativity can significantly lift your mood and pull you out from the slump of anxiety or depression that often accompanies negative thinking.

Employ Positive Affirmations

Positive affirmations are statements that are meant to help you overcome negative thoughts and they challenge you to believe in yourself. When you repeat these statements to yourself regularly, they become imprinted on your consciousness, and you begin to realize the truthfulness in them. Reciting positive affirmations can not only help you to get rid of uncomfortable negative thoughts, but it can also motivate you to start acting positively in order to achieve the outcomes you desire. Furthermore, positive affirmations can help you alleviate the effects of stress and anxiety that comes from overthinking about negative things. Just like workout exercises, positive affirmations trigger the release of feel-good hormones in the body and increase the generation of new clusters of "positive thought" neurons in the brain.

If you are struggling with negative thinking cycles, here are some of the best positive affirmations that you can repeat to yourself in order to begin thinking more positively:

- I am in control of my life today, and I choose to think positively today.
- I refuse to allow negative thoughts to rob me of my peace of mind.
- I am enough and I possess all the qualities to direct my life as I please.
- I am powerful enough to conquer any challenges which I may face today.
- I acknowledge my uniqueness and the talents which I possess.
- I am strong enough to face this day with an open heart and clarity of mind.

Take a Walk

Staying in one place for too long can make you feel grumpy and anxious, which often triggers negative thinking. Sometimes all that is needed to reset the mind is a simple walk in another location. When you feel like negative thoughts are distracting you, one of the best ways of clearing the mind is to take a stroll in a scenic place. There are plenty of great places where you can go for a walk whenever you feel assailed by negative thinking. Parks and forests are good places to start. Of course, it's nice if you have access to parks and other beautiful places, but any location will do, as long as you get out and get moving. If you live in a place where there are none of these, you can still go on a walk in or near your neighborhood. It is advisable to avoid crowded streets and busy commercial places since the noise and bustle of activity can be uncomfortable when you are feeling negative.

Keep a Gratitude Journal

Very often, we get so caught up in our lives and the challenges that we are facing that we end up losing focus on all the ways in which life has been kind to us. Just because you are experiencing a challenging situation at present doesn't mean there's nothing good going for you in your life. So, when you get stuck in a cycle of negative thinking, it is a good idea to take a step back and take an inventory of how life has been good to you.

Rather than focus on the negative thoughts running through your mind, create a gratitude journal and list all the things you are grateful for in your life. These may include good health, a career that you enjoy, meaningful friendships and relationships in your life, and so much more. Record the good things that have happened and the things that have given you joy recently. Remember that nothing is too small or too big when it comes to gratitude. Even something as trivial as having an easy day at work can be something to be thankful for. Maybe you saw a beautiful bird, or someone held a door for you. Take the time to list everything in your life that you are happy about or thankful for, regardless of how small or insignificant it may seem. Keep in mind that sometimes the best things in our lives are right in front of our eyes waiting for us to notice them.

Approaching your negative thinking with gratitude can help you develop a greater appreciation of your life. Gratitude for what we have helps us view situations more positively no matter how challenging they may seem.

Change Your Environment

It is very easy for us to become so accustomed to a particular location that we become weary and bored of it. This can lead to feelings of restlessness and may trigger negative thoughts that we cannot escape. If you are feeling overwhelmed by negative thinking, a change of scenery can help you clear your mind of negative thoughts. This does not mean you have to permanently move to a different location. A simple act such as spending a few hours somewhere different, especially if it is a beautiful spot such as a park, can work wonders in terms of providing you with relief. You might also have a favorite coffee spot or a nicely decorated part of a mall or a community center that you like. Use these places to spend time away from home or work and bring variety to your life. You will be able to relax your mind and be able to think more clearly.

Engage in Workout Exercises

As we discussed in the introduction of this book, anxiety is one of the most common causes of negative thinking. In some cases, this anxiety arises out of pent up tension in the body and mind. One way of releasing all this frustration and tension in the body is to engage in workout exercises. There are numerous benefits to exercising whenever you feel overwhelmed by anxiety or negativity. One of the advantages of keeping yourself active by working out is that it triggers the release of feel-good endorphins such as dopamine and serotonin, which can greatly lift your mood. Working out also enhances blood circulation in the body, and can help alleviate symptoms of stress and depression.

Studies have shown that regular exercise can significantly improve one's cognitive processes. You don't need to engage in intensive fitness training at a gym. Even simply taking a few minutes to jog, walk or get on your exercise machine can significantly improve blood flow in the brain and help clear your thoughts. So, next time you feel assailed by negative thoughts, take a moment to stretch, do exercises or even go for a short walk or jog? If you are in an apartment or office building, climb a few flights of stairs. Your body and mind will surely thank you for it.

Practice Deep Breathing

Deep breathing is a very effective way of clearing your mind of negative thoughts. This is because when you breathe deeply, it signals your brain to relax. This message is then relayed to your body, telling it to relax. Performing deep breathing exercises allows your body and mind to calm down whenever you find yourself overthinking. By practicing deep breathing, you allow your body to release any tension that you may be experiencing. This can help you ease any anxiety or stress you may be feeling. When you feel overwhelmed by negative thoughts, take a few minutes to perform a routine of deep breathing. Draw in controlled deep breaths through your nostrils and expel all the air (slowly) from your diaphragm. Doing so will help you feel calm and relaxed almost instantly.

Employ Humor

It is often said that laughter is the best medicine, and this certainly rings true when it comes to dealing with negative thinking. Laughter, just like fitness exercises, is known to release feel-good hormones, which can help lift your mood whenever you are feeling overwhelmed with negative thoughts. Of course, it can be very difficult to bring yourself to laugh when your mind is constantly being bombarded with uncomfortable thoughts every minute of your day. However, using humor to counter your negative thinking is very effective, and produces positive results almost instantly.

Therefore, whenever you feel like life is happening faster than you can keep up with, or you are feeling overwhelmed by negativity, you can derive a lot of comfort by taking a step back and laughing at the quirkiness of it all. Watch a show that is funny, and even if you don't feel like it, make a point to laugh at it. The action of laughter will release those feel-good hormones.

Remember not to take life so seriously all the time, since this negatively impacts how much you are able to enjoy it.

Summary

Negative thoughts can seem very overwhelming and cause you to feel like you are losing control over yourself and your life; however, it is possible to overcome them. With the right strategies and practices, you can clear your mind of negative thinking and regain your self-confidence (Bloom, 2015).

In this chapter, we learned about the many ways we can clear our mind of negative thoughts. In summary, here are the things you need to do whenever you feel overwhelmed by negative thoughts.

- Pay close attention to your body language and readjust any aspects that may be triggering your negative thoughts.
- Share your uncomfortable thoughts and emotions with someone you trust.
- Take a few moments to relax and calm your mind such that you begin to view your negative thoughts from an objective state of mind.
- Try to gain a different perspective of your negative thinking by looking at it from a new point of view.
- Use your anxiety and frustration as forces for good by channeling them towards creation. Painting, writing and composing music can act as outlets for your negative thoughts.
- Take frequent walks in serene environments to relax your mind whenever you feel bombarded by too much negative thinking.
- Recognize, focus on and be grateful for all the good things you have going for you in your life, no matter how insignificant they may seem.
- Spend some time in your favorite outdoor and indoor locations where you feel comfortable and relaxed. This can help calm your mind whenever you spiral into negative thinking and overthinking.
- Exercise in order to give your body an outlet for anxiety and stress. This will relax your body and mind when you feel assailed by negative thoughts. This can be as simple as jogging for a few

minutes, climbing some stairs or performing some stretching exercises.

- Practice deep breathing exercises to release tension in your body and mind whenever you feel overwhelmed by negative thoughts. This helps you to attain some clarity of mind.
- Use laughter to counter your negative thinking; you should not take life so seriously all the time.

In this chapter, you learned about the different methods you can use to clear your mind of negative thoughts. I have no doubt in my mind that you now have all the tools to help you counter negative thinking whenever it arises in your day to day life.

In the next chapter, you will learn some of the ways you can deal with the problem of negative thinking and permanently eliminate it from your life. If you have noticed that you have a tendency of obsessing over your negative thoughts more than you should, and you want to stop this behavior for good, then this next chapter is going to be very helpful for you.

CHAPTER THREE:

Eliminate the Bad Habit of Negative Thinking for Good

If you constantly struggle to overcome negative thinking, you might worry that there is something inherently wrong with you. However, this couldn't be further from the truth. Negative thinking is a normal part of being human. Over the course of our evolution, we naturally developed this trait as a survival strategy. Being aware of the negative potential in a situation or environment can help us become more aware of the issues that threaten our survival. This means anyone can be trapped in a cycle of pessimistic thinking at some point in their lives.

Although negative thinking is innate in us as human beings and can often be a motivator for us to act, when the thoughts become too intense and too frequent, they can interfere with our lives. It is therefore important not to allow your negative thinking to develop into a habit. Nevertheless, if you feel like you have already sunk into a hole of pessimism and negative thinking, this does not mean that you are doomed! As a matter of fact, there are several ways that you can rein in your negative thinking and eliminate it for good.

This chapter will present useful tools to help you eliminate the bad habit of negative thinking from your life for good.

Recognize and Step Back from Negative Thought Patterns

If you are constantly bombarded by negative thoughts that are intrusive, you know just how stressful they can be. That is why you need to take immediate steps to neutralize negative thinking patterns.

The first thing you can do in this regard is to recognize the loops of negative thinking that you often get stuck in and to take a step back to view them from a detached state of mind (O'Brien, 2019b). Easier said than done, right? Actually, gaining awareness of your negative thinking patterns is very simple to do as long as you have the right tools. The primary tool you require to achieve this is "cognitive defusion". The process of cognitive defusion is probably something you are already familiar with, you just don't realize it.

What is Cognitive Defusion and How is it Helpful?

Cognitive defusion is a mental process that is commonly associated with Acceptance and Commitment Therapy (ACT). Essentially, defusion is based on the idea that taking our thoughts too literally can lead to mental and psychological problems. Cognitive defusion techniques are designed to put our thoughts together with our experiences in order to allow for the distinction between the two to be recognized.

To better understand how cognitive defusion works, let us consider how our minds work. Generally, in our day to day lives, everything we experience or see is subject to labeling, categorization, evaluation, and comparison. This is a process that unfolds automatically, and it is facilitated by our cognitive analysis functions. This means that all these processes happen even without our conscious awareness, which is very useful when it comes to problem-solving.

However, a problem arises when these mental processes that facilitate comparison and pass judgment are directed inwards. This typically yields negative judgments upon ourselves and causes us to become hypercritical of ourselves and others. Eventually, when these processes merge with our psyche, we begin associating with them in a manner that is not reflective of reality. This results in problems such as overthinking and intrusive negative thoughts.

The aim of cognitive defusion is to allow us to recognize these processes without forming an attachment to them. It enables us to form partnerships with our thoughts (both negative and positive) without ceding control over our lives to them. This mindset requires that we do not suppress or try to deflect our thoughts, but rather observe them and acknowledge them from a distance. By developing cognitive defusion, we are able to distinguish the thoughts that are workable from those that are not. Unproductive thoughts are encouraged because they help us to pursue our visions and aspirations in life. On the other hand, thoughts that are not productive or positive are only meant to be observed and acknowledged but not acted upon since they lead us nowhere. They can be considered and then treated as background noise.

There are several skills that are involved in the process of cognitive defusion. These include:

- The ability to evaluate whether a thought is workable and productive. Does it align with your values and aspirations in life?
- Developing an acute ability to view thoughts simply as mental impressions rather than tangible things that exist in reality. This skill is very valuable because it enables us to be less caught up or entangled in our thoughts, particularly the negative ones.

Cognitive defusion is a very important skill to develop since it can be applied in various ways. Some of the scenarios where this skill can come in handy include:

- When you have patterns of thought that are repetitive or recurrent, especially if they have to do with your opinion or perception of yourself. For instance, "I'm not good enough" or "I will not amount to anything." These thoughts may seem benign and harmless at first, but once they take root in your mind, they can lead to anxiety and self-doubt which can result in negativity.

- When you are unable to determine the accuracy of our thoughts (also known as cognitive restructuring). Cognitive defusion can help reduce the psychological impact of thoughts without altering their content or frequency.

- When your negative thoughts become barriers to your progress. Sometimes when we are about to take a risk towards something that we actually want, we are plagued by thoughts such as, "What if I fail?" or "I'm not talented enough." Through cognitive defusion, we can bypass these thoughts so that we act in ways that will catapult us towards the things we desire, even if it involves taking risks.

- When we are faced with a serious problem which we should otherwise be dealing with in a realistic way. Cognitive defusion can help us alleviate the stress of opening up to the possibilities that exist in situations that may seem very daunting.

There are various techniques that are employed in cognitive defusion. These techniques can be applied to any stream of thought, although they are most helpful when one is faced with intrusive negative thoughts.

The first thing you need to do when applying cognitive defusion is to think about a negative thought that you are constantly plagued by. This could be something like, "I am not worthy enough," or "I will never succeed at this." Once you have identified the negative thought, focus on it for a moment in order to get in fusion with it, then make that thought the target of your cognitive defusion practice. Here are some of the techniques which you will need to apply.

Recognize and Acknowledge

The first thing you need to do when applying cognitive defusion is to recognize and acknowledge the negative thoughts. This entails adding a cognition phrase such as, "I notice I am having the thought..." to the repetitive uncomfortable thought. Doing this will allow you to alter your relationship with your difficult thoughts.

Name It To Tame It - Assign a Label to Your Thoughts

Very often, we get trapped in our cycles of negative thinking because we try to fight or argue with negative thoughts, or we try to push them away. However, trying to cope with negative thoughts in these ways only amplifies them, and further reinforces their power over our lives.

So, how do we deal with the negative thoughts that plague us in a way that is effective and practical? The "name it to tame it" technique will help free you from negative thinking loops without having to fight them (O'Brien, 2019b). Here is how it works:

Once you recognize and acknowledge your negative thoughts, the next thing you need to do is label them. You can approach this technique in two different ways.

Your thoughts usually fall into the category of evaluative or descriptive. Descriptive thoughts are those that are related to our direct sensory experience, such as things we see, hear or touch. Evaluative thoughts, on the other hand, consider our experience and are mostly based on concepts such as good-bad, right-wrong.

When observing your thoughts, you should be able to label them depending on what kind of thoughts they are. For example, is the negative thought that you are having an image, a question or a statement of blame? Once you have identified and labeled your recurring negative thought, you can give it a label to address it whenever it pops into your head. You may have already noticed that most of our negative thoughts are recurrent, and usually involve the same storylines, such as, "I'm not good enough to succeed." You might respond to yourself by saying, "There's my self-blaming thought," or "There's my fear of inadequacy again." whenever such a thought appears in your mind. This allows you to create distance from your thought, and perceive it as something conceptual rather than actual. The goal is to realize that it's only just a thought, and it doesn't necessarily reflect reality. Once you have assigned the label, simply try to "let it go". Give it a name, and then put it in the background while you consider other ways to think of the situation you are in. In doing so, you prevent the negative thought from overwhelming your mental state and mood.

Appreciate Your Mind

The idea here is to refrain from giving your negative thoughts too much importance since this creates tension and struggle. Give it a moment of consideration and then put it aside. Whenever that recurring thought pops into your mind, you need to "appreciate" or "thank" your mind for giving you that thought, but in a kind of sarcastic tone similar to how you would respond to a nagging teenager who says something provocative to trigger a reaction out of you. For example, tell your mind, "Yes, yes, I know, very scary, it could all go wrong. Got it." Be thankful that you have been informed of that potential outcome, and then consider other more positive perspectives of the situation.

Mindful Observation

Mindful observation involves considering your thoughts with an attitude of curiosity and openness. Spend some time observing your flow of thoughts without trying to analyze or judge them. This might be challenging to do since our minds are naturally designed to evaluate things, including our own thoughts. However, if you notice that you are trying too hard to analyze your thoughts, take note of that and then continue to observe the thoughts that follow.

There are various images that may help you become good at mindful observation. For instance, you can think of your thoughts as boats floating on a lake. In this case, the lake represents your mind, while your thoughts are represented by the boats. Try to observe your thoughts the same way you would watch the boats gliding peacefully over the lake. Similarly, images of birds soaring effortlessly through the sky is another image you could use.

Approaching mindful observation using these images will help you overcome the tendency to negatively analyze, evaluate and judge your thoughts. It will allow you to observe your thoughts with a sense of curiosity and detachment, thus helping you to achieve relaxation and peace.

Come to Your Senses

If you pay close attention to your negative thoughts, you may already be aware that most of them arise from one of two sources.

The first is an obsession over the past. Perhaps you spend a lot of time thinking about past actions which you regret, circumstances that didn't turn out as you had hoped, or bad things that happened to you. This can result in a perpetual feeling of guilt and sadness, and make you predisposed to negative thinking.

The second factor that contributes to negative thinking is constant anxiety about the future. As humans, we are naturally prone to experience fear about the uncertainty of life. Maybe you find yourself worrying about the future of your family, relationships or career. This can put you in a state of constant worry and negativity.

When you investigate your negative thinking loops carefully, you will realize that your mind is focused on the future or past.

The problem with these negative thought patterns is that they steal our focus away from the real world. When you get too invested in them, you lose track of your life. You may also end up losing connection with the people in your life and the world in which you live.

In order to begin living in the present, you need to divert your attention from your negative thoughts and direct your attention to the world around you. You can do this by practicing the "coming to your senses" technique. The technique involves redirecting your attention away from your thoughts and focusing on your senses. Be aware of your surroundings, and focus on what is happening. What can you hear, what can you see? How does it relate to your situation at that moment? You will experience a greater awareness of yourself and the world around you. You will also gain a sense of calm and relaxation which will help ground you when plagued with difficult thoughts.

Helpful Questions

Negative thinking patterns tend to be very relentless. No matter how hard you try to overcome them, they can persist. If you find yourself plagued by negative thoughts, there are several tools that you can use to unshackle yourself and change your situation. These tools are in the form of questions that are used in Acceptance and Commitment Therapy (ACT). The questions are designed to help you challenge your negative thoughts in order to shift your focus.

The best approach to this method involved asking yourself questions and answering them in your head (O'Brien, 2019b). Here are some of the questions you need to consider in order to overcome negative thinking patterns.

- Is this thought helpful or useful to me in any way?
- Is this thought grounded in reality?
- Is this thought important or is my mind just engaging in mental chatter?
- Does this thought help me to take action towards achieving my objectives?

Once you ask and respond to these helpful questions, you can follow up with some positive questions that will help you redirect your focus towards constructive thoughts. Ideally, you should handle these questions one at a time and only move to the next one after you've sufficiently answered the one before it.

- What do I consider to be true?
- What outcome will I get out of this situation, and how can I make it happen?
- What should I do to make the best out of this situation?
- Will I be better off without this thought?
- What are some of the things I can focus on now?

- Can I view this from a different point of view?
- What can I be grateful for at this moment?

Asking and answering these questions can change your perspective and redirect your attention from your negative thoughts to the potential of positivity in your everyday reality.

Summary

In this chapter, we have looked at some of the tools and techniques that can help you overcome your negative thinking patterns and take back power and control over the way we think. Whenever you feel overwhelmed with uncomfortable thought patterns, remember to:

- Use cognitive defusion to distinguish between the thoughts in your head and the reality of your situation. This will allow you to develop a positive relationship with your thoughts. It will also enable you to view your thoughts from a point of calm detachment, rather than allowing the thoughts to govern your emotions and actions.
- Learn and practice the "name it to tame it" technique. This will help you to break free from negative thought patterns without having to struggle with them.
- Be in the present by focusing your attention away from your negative thoughts and direct them to your sense perceptions of your immediate situation. This will provide you with relief by calming your mind and freeing you of worries about the past or the future.
- Use "helpful questions" to dig deep into your thoughts and determine their veracity. You may also use follow up questions to challenge your negative thoughts and replace them with positive ones.

This chapter has focused on giving you tools and techniques to deal with negative thoughts in an effective manner. The strategies we have discussed have been proven to work. If you struggle perpetually with negative thinking, start practicing these strategies. This will help you to eliminate the negative thought patterns you are faced with and assist you to regain control of your thinking.

In the next chapter, you are going to learn how to take control of your thinking and prevent yourself from spiraling into negativity. This next chapter is undoubtedly one of the most crucial in this book, as it will show you how to nip negative thinking in the bud before it grows into a bigger problem. Pay close attention to our pointers. They will be invaluable to your strategy for eliminating negative thinking permanently.

CHAPTER FOUR:

How to Control Your Thoughts and Stop Spiralling into Negativity

Depression and anxiety are often characterized by negative thoughts that can be difficult to deal with. People often don't realize just how serious their negative thinking is affecting them until it's too late. However, even if your negative thinking has become habitual, there are mental strategies that you can employ to help you take control of your thought process. Let us examine some of these strategies and see how we can use them to deal with negative thoughts.

Making a Mental Shift

In order to take control of your thought process and prevent negative thoughts from taking hold in your mind, you need to make a conscious effort to shift your thinking. This can be very challenging to do; however, with regular practice, it will soon become second nature to you, and you will be able to shift your thinking without making a lot of effort.

So, what does making a mental shift involve? Basically, shifting your mental focus entails challenging your established perception about a difficult situation. It requires you to consider whatever worries you may be facing and directing your attention towards something different. The aim of mental shifting is to break the cycle of unwanted or uncomfortable recurring thoughts (Elmer, 2019).

A key component of this strategy involves reversing the negative thoughts that you may have picked up from other people. For instance, if you have been brought up to believe that you have to excel in academia in order to have a good future, you might feel like a failure if you do not achieve this. Holding onto these beliefs might make you very susceptible to negative thinking. This is why you need to unlearn such beliefs if you hope to get rid of the negative thought patterns you are prone to.

By deliberately shifting your focus away from negative thoughts, you can significantly alleviate anxiety and stress and free yourself from uncomfortable thought loops.

Do Your Thoughts Include Should?

When learning how to make a mental shift you must identify the common thought loops that you get caught up in, and learn how to recognize negative thinking instantly. For instance, if your thought process includes the word "should", you need to evaluate why you think in that way. For instance, you might be having a thought loop that tells you, "I should do a certain thing," or "I should not feel a particular way." Although these thoughts might be well-intentioned, they can elicit feelings of guilt and pull you into a spiral of negative thinking.

A great way of countering thoughts like these is to change the words you use to take account of your imperfection and limitations as a human being. Instead of thinking "I should not feel this way," you can instead say, " I don't feel well right now due to the challenges I'm experiencing, but I'm sure it will pass." By shifting your approach in this way, the pressure might be significantly lifted.

To make a successful mental shift when plagued by negative thoughts, you also need to identify any patterns of negative thinking that you might be caught up in. In most cases, thoughts that express commands, such as I "should", emerge out of mental distortions referred to as automatic negative thinking.

Negative thoughts that arise due to automatic negative thinking are usually reflective of strong aversions we may have towards certain things. These thoughts tend to develop into habits and become persistent, which makes them very difficult to deal with. They are usually very common if one is struggling with anxiety or depression.

Automatic negative thinking isn't always easy to recognize since it usually develops over a long period. Most people usually don't even realize that this is the cause of their negative thoughts unless someone else points it out to them. However, you can identify these patterns of thinking by maintaining records of your thoughts.

You can go about this in the following way:

- Identify the situation that you are in.
- Recognize and note any emotions that you might be experiencing.
- Pay attention to the images or thoughts that come to mind.

Here are the steps you need to follow to figure out if your negative thoughts stem from automatic negative thinking.

1. Assess the Situation

The first thing you need to do is to evaluate the situation you find yourself in. Some of the leading questions that may aid you in this evaluation include:

- Which people are involved in this situation?
- Where did this incident take place?
- What did I do to find myself in this position?
- When did this incident happen?

2. Evaluate Your Mood and Feelings

You will need to record any emotions you may be experiencing as a result of the situation. For example, are you angry, nervous or sad? It is also a good idea to note down the degree to which you feel affected.

You can use percentages or other scales to denote this. For example, today I feel 75% sad, or my sadness is a 7 out of 10. Don't worry too much about getting the percentages exactly correct. You can choose any figure depending on the extent to which you feel those particular emotions. The key here is to trust your instincts and to take time to evaluate your moods and feelings.

3. Record the Automatic Thoughts that are Going Through Your Mind

The final and most important step in this process is to note down the automatic thoughts that are running through your head. These may include thoughts such as:

- I am stupid.
- I am overreacting.
- I can't deal with this.

If you realize that you are manifesting such automatic negative thoughts, you should deconstruct the situation to make it more manageable. This will allow you to make a shift of perspective and prevent your negative thinking from affecting your mood.

You need to investigate the reasoning behind your negative thinking to figure out why the situation you are in makes you think that way. For instance, if your negative thinking story says "I will never be a good parent", you may ask yourself whether this thought stems from the way in which you were brought up by your parents. It is important to follow this thought process to its logical conclusion since this will provide you with great insights into why you are prone to such negative thoughts about yourself.

It can also be worthwhile to imagine the worst-case scenario and take note of the feelings it arouses in you. When you evaluate your situation with honesty and an open mind, you might find out that your beliefs about yourself are totally unfounded, and that you have no reason to be anxious.

Once you have identified your automatic negative thoughts, you need to scrutinize them to see whether they hold true. You may come to the realization that there is no evidence whatsoever to support your train of thought. Even if there is some evidence that is based on past experiences, it might not be exactly applicable in your current situation.

Therefore, when investigating your automatic negative thinking loops, you need to give emphasis to credible evidence rather than emotions. Weigh all the evidence before making a judgment on whether your thought is grounded in rationality or is just another symptom of anxiety. If you determine that your thought is irrational, you can then replace it with a new one that factors in all the sound evidence, and one that allows your rational mind to take charge of your thinking.

When dealing with stressful automatic negative thinking, it is also important to acknowledge when you feel overwhelmed by your thoughts. People are quick to react defensively when they encounter difficult thoughts that they are unable to control. This is not only ineffective but can also be very counterproductive. Trying to fight your thoughts only makes them persist, which can hurl you down a spiral of anxiety. Regardless of where your negative thoughts come from, the first thing you need to do to overcome them is to welcome them carefully into your mind space. This is by no means an easy thing to do. After all, no one enjoys being bombarded by negative thoughts constantly. However, by carefully embracing your uncomfortable thoughts, you significantly reduce mental strain and expend less energy than you would do trying to fight them. Rather than spending all your efforts struggling with the negative thoughts, consider the possibility that they are there to teach you something. I assure you, once you learn that stressful thoughts are there for a reason, you will be better equipped to manage the feelings of anxiety and frustration that they elicit.

Summary

In this chapter, you learned that in order to control your thoughts and stop spiraling into negativity, you need to make a mental shift. There are several main takeaways from this chapter. When it comes to dealing with negative thinking habits, here are some important things to keep in mind.

- Making a mental shift is vital to getting rid of negative thoughts for good. To do so, you must be able to challenge your negative thoughts and determine their plausibility. To achieve this, you need to redirect your thoughts from the negative story in your head and replace that with a different perspective which takes into account the facts of the situation.
- Thoughts that include the word "should" are very challenging to deal with since they create intense pressure, which has to be resolved. If you are making "should" statements to yourself, you need to break down your thinking patterns in order to make navigating such thoughts easier. Generally, thoughts such as these reflect automatic negative thinking which develops over time. It is therefore important to scrutinize these thoughts to determine whether they are backed by evidence or are simply mental chatter arising from long developed habits (Elmer, 2019).

Learning how to identify and evaluate automatic negative thinking patterns is very crucial to making a mental shift away from negative thinking. If you have been struggling with these thoughts, developing these skills can prove to be invaluable. In most cases, negative thinking tends to go hand-in-hand with overthinking, which can also be a major problem. Obsessively thinking about negative thoughts can seriously affect your mood.

In the next chapter, we are going to look at some of the strategies you can employ to deal with overthinking and overcome the tendency of obsessing over your negative thoughts. By the end of the chapter, you should be able to easily recognize how your overthinking habits arise and use various techniques to troubleshoot this problem.

CHAPTER FIVE:

How to Stop Overthinking

Overthinking is a common problem affecting people across all age groups. While it is normal to obsess over some thoughts once in a while, when you spend all your time ruminating over your thoughts, it can become a serious problem.

Overthinking typically happens when you obsess over the past or become anxious about the future. Unlike regular thinking which is geared towards problem-solving, overthinking just makes you dwell on the problem without providing any solutions (Oppong, 2020). It is normal and even beneficial to think deeply during moments of self-reflection since this allows you to gain important insights that you can use to solve the problems you are facing. However, overthinking only makes you feel powerless about your situation and does not serve any meaningful purpose.

Unfortunately, in most cases, it is not easy to tell whether you are actually engaging in overthinking. Some people might confuse overthinking with self-reflection since both involve spending a significant amount of time thinking about something. However, the difference between the two is that self-reflection leads to useful insights, whereas overthinking only drains your energy and time. It doesn't matter how long you spend overthinking. You are unlikely to find a solution to whatever problem you are experiencing. It is therefore important to recognize when you are engaging in overthinking and learn how to stop it from cluttering your mind.

Here are some of the signs that you may be overthinking:

- You can't stop yourself from thinking about a negative incident that happened in the past.
- You find yourself engaging in negative thinking very often.
- You tend to focus on the worst-case scenario in any kind of situation.
- You tend to obsess over past mistakes and failures even though they may have no bearing on your current life.
- You tend to overanalyze every detail of your everyday interactions with other people.
- You often relive any embarrassing moments you may have had in the past.
- You find it difficult to sleep because your mind won't shut off.
- You spend a lot of time looking for hidden meaning in what others say. You might even overinflate some statements and their possible meanings.
- You spend significant amounts of time worrying about things that you have absolutely no control over.

Overthinking is certainly a serious problem that can be damaging to your self-esteem and peace of mind. However, just because you are afflicted by constant negative thoughts doesn't mean you should give up. There are several steps outlined below that you can take to reclaim a sense of control over your life and overcome the problem of overthinking for good.

Develop an Awareness of the Problem

By now, you probably understand that most of the thoughts we have occur spontaneously and automatically. In the previous chapter, we looked at how our automatic negative thoughts arise out of habits we have developed unconsciously over the course of our lives. Usually, these thoughts latch onto our minds and become repetitive, thus making it impossible to make progress in our lives. The first step in overcoming overthinking, therefore, is to be aware of your thoughts. You must begin to view your thoughts from the perspective of an outside observer in order to avoid becoming attached to them.

Becoming the observer entails more than just identifying your thoughts. In essence, you need to become aware of the sensations and feelings that accompany your negative thoughts. This is because our thoughts happen automatically, and may capture all our attention at the time. They emerge and dissipate often at lightning speeds, making it very difficult for us to focus on a single thought process and follow it down to its genesis. Nevertheless, with constant practice, self-observation is a skill that is very possible to learn.

Learning how to observe and evaluate your negative thinking from a neutral or objective point of view allows you to gain a different perspective. You will be able to understand the source of your negative thoughts and how they affect your emotions and moods. You will also be able to pick up on any counterproductive defensive mechanisms which you normally resort to when plagued with difficult recurrent thoughts. Learning how to observe your obsessive thought patterns also enables you to realize that your thoughts arise all by themselves. This realization allows you to see your thoughts from a more accepting and objective point of view. This can provide you with a lot of relief and peace of mind whenever you find yourself obsessively overthinking something negative.

Understand Your Triggers

Overthinking is a problem that profoundly affects our emotional health. That is because we rarely overthink all the positive things in our lives. Overthinking is usually rooted in a negative memory or concern. Therefore, in order to deal with constant ruminating in an effective manner, it is vital to recognize and understand the emotional triggers that lead you to overthink. Emotional triggers refer to the words, actions, opinions, situations, people, etc. that arouse strong negative emotion in you. When you are triggered, you may experience a range of emotions, including fear, anger, sadness, and rage. These emotions may, in turn, cause you to overthink the scenario. There are various reasons why you may be emotionally triggered. These include:

1. Past Trauma

An individual who has experienced a very traumatic event in the past might get triggered when they see, hear, smell, touch or taste something that reminds them of their negative experience. For instance, a person who was abused as a child by their caregivers might be triggered when they see parents who have a bad relationship with their child. Similarly, an individual whose spouse died of lung cancer due to smoking tobacco might feel triggered by the smell of cigarettes or whenever they see someone smoking.

Post-traumatic triggers are usually a symptom that one's trauma has not been resolved. Fortunately, this can be solved through guided behavioral therapy, which aims to help victims understand their triggers and develop effective ways of coping with them.

2. Conflicting Beliefs and Values

As human beings, we tend to adhere to and defend our beliefs vigorously. The belief systems which we learned and adapted to over the course of our lives play a crucial role in shaping our values. This subsequently shapes the way we think and behave. When we identify too strongly with a particular belief, we may find it difficult to be tolerant of other people's beliefs, especially if they contradict our own. This is why religion creates so much conflict and discord in society. Our beliefs provide us with a sense of comfort and safety in the challenging world we live in. So, when they are challenged, we may feel as if the entire basis of our lives has come under threat. When other people question our beliefs and values, we are likely to see this as an attack on our personhood. However, it is important to realize that belief systems, even the most enduring ones, are not set in stone. They are subject to change over time as we acquire new information and experiences.

3. Preservation of our Ego

If you possess any basic understanding of modern psychology, you may be familiar with the concept of the "ego". Essentially, the ego is the distinct sense of selfhood that every human being carries with them throughout life. It is a confluence of many things, including our preconceived thoughts and notions, cultural values, upbringing, belief systems, memories, desires, and habits. The primary purpose is to perpetuate our experience of self-hood and shield us from experiencing the death of our familiar selves. So the ego creates a network of ideas, thoughts, beliefs, and habits through which we derive our sense of identity. It is therefore not surprising that whenever our sense of identity is challenged by others, we are likely to become triggered instantly. When someone hurts us, our egos immediately spring to action in a bid to defend our identity. Some of the ways we may respond include arguing, insulting, defaming or belittling the object of our anger. In extreme cases, some people may commit serious crimes such as assault or murder when they feel that their ego is under threat. This just goes to prove how powerful this aspect of our lives actually is. However, while the ego can be very destructive, it can also be a force for good when kept in balance. After all, the ego is an integral aspect of every human being.

Every human being has an ego. The fact that we do not see a high percentage of people committing serious crimes is because a balanced ego is a desirable, beneficial and somewhat common thing. Therefore, if you have a problem dealing with people or ideas that challenge your ego, you need to learn how to keep your ego healthy so that you can accept the perspectives of others without feeling threatened. Some of the practices that might help you do so include meditation, introspection and performing acts of service to others.

By understanding how the ego works and developing a healthy ego, you can overcome the triggers that make you susceptible to overthinking.

Focus on the Big Picture

Very often, we get caught up in the small worries and anxieties of our day-to-day lives, to a point where we get sidetracked from our biggest goals. As a matter of fact, most goals in life, whether in career or relationships, take some time before they can be realized. Therefore, the longer this period is prolonged, the easier it is to lose sight of the big picture. When you focus too much on the small details affecting your ambitions, you inevitably end up with less time to think about your ultimate goals. This can have a detrimental effect on your overall drive and enthusiasm. In some cases, you may end up forgetting about your goal completely, as your mind gets distracted by immediate worries and problems. In order to maintain the integrity of your aspirations and goals, it is essential to remind yourself of the big picture.

How can you do this? Well, the secret to focusing on your big goals is to bring them back to your conscious awareness. In essence, you need to constantly remind yourself of your personal vision in life. There are several strategies that can help you to regularly recall your mission and focus on the big picture. Here are some of the tips you can employ towards this end.

1. Set Aside Some Time Every Week to Engage in Planning

You need to dedicate some hours every week to think about your goals and your overarching mission in life. The aim of doing this is to remind yourself of your aspirations and pull yourself away from all the minute distractions that may sideline you from working on your ultimate goals in life.

2. Devise a Symbol that Reminds You of Your Mission

It is essential to come up with a symbol that reminds you of your goals in life. You may choose to draw the symbol yourself if you are artistically gifted, or you can simply select one from the public domain that resonates with you and aligns with your goals. For instance, if you are an aspiring musician, you can use a music symbol, images of your mentors or other people you look up to as your symbols. Whatever or whoever you select for your symbol is entirely up to you. Print that symbol and set it in a location where it is likely to capture your attention easily. You can stick the image above your bed, on the door to your room, on your desk or even make it into a pendant which you can wear frequently. Every time you see the symbol, you will be reminded of your goals.

3. Give Yourself a Break

Sometimes we get so caught up in our careers and social lives that the positive and creative energy in us becomes sapped. This can lead to performance problems, which may end up leaving us frustrated and overwhelmed with negative thoughts. It is therefore very important to take frequent breaks to replenish and rejuvenate your mind so that you can begin working optimally again. If you are experiencing negative thoughts due to burnout, it might be wise to set aside some time to unwind. This will help you reboot and declutter your mind so that your thinking and creativity flow more freely.

4. Eliminate All Distractions when Planning for Your Goals

You are advised to steer clear of any possible distractions whenever you are planning for your goals. Ideally, you should find a quiet place with few distractions in order to be able to think more clearly when working out your plans for the future. Set aside time to focus on yourself and what you want to achieve.

5. Write Down Your Goals and Read Them Often

Committing to your goals in writing creates a personal contract, and allows you to connect with your mission statement more fully. You don't need to write an entire book describing everything in detail. A two-to-three sentence summary that captures the essence of your mission statement should be more than enough. It can even be a list in point form. Once you come up with your mission and commit to it in writing, practice reading it to yourself at least twice a day, especially in the morning when you wake up and just before you go to bed. Doing so will keep your goals at the forefront of your mind at all times, even as you navigate the minute challenges of your day-to-day life.

Realize that Chronic Overthinking is Not Permanent

When you are caught up in the cycle of overthinking, it is easy to think that this is a challenge you'll never be able to overcome. This gloomy mindset can make you very depressed and hopeless. It can also lead you to make counterproductive decisions to combat your negative thinking, hence compounding the problem.

However, just because you are dealing with constant negative thoughts doesn't mean you are doomed forever! Chronic overthinking does not have to be permanent. By changing your mindset from resignation to determination, you can begin to investigate the problem and find an effective way to move forward.

Minimize Your Daily Input

One of the main reasons why we fall into the trap of overthinking is because we expose ourselves to too much information. In the age that we live in, we are constantly bombarded by vast amounts of information coming from various sources. These sources include television, the internet and social media sites like Facebook and Twitter. This unrelenting overload of information clutters our mind with useless facts which serve no purpose other than to clog our mind and distract us from the reality of our lives.

When your mind gets jammed with too much information, you may find yourself spending copious amounts of time ruminating over issues that are not remotely relevant to your life. This can seriously upset your mental balance and affect very essential aspects of your life, including daily happiness and sleep. In order to get rid of the tendency to overthink, therefore, it is absolutely vital that you minimize the amount of information you expose yourself to on a day-to-day basis. For instance, try to cut down the amount of time you spend browsing the internet and checking social media notifications and messages. In addition to this, try to abstain from using your phone just before bedtime. This will help you avoid information that may affect your sleep.

Reconnect with the Immediate World

If you spend most of your time overthinking and worrying, you may end up living in your head too much and fail to experience the vibrant and exciting world that is happening around you. Constantly obsessing over the minute details of your negative thoughts robs you of the opportunity to actually connect with your environment and the people in it. Overthinking can cause you to live in your head so much that you lose track of the real world. In essence, when you are constantly worrying about the minute worries in your life, you may end up losing track of the most important things in your life.

Develop an awareness of your overthinking habits to prevent the tendency of living in your head too much, and take active steps to reconnect with the immediate world.

Redirecting your focus from obsessive negative thoughts and channeling your energy towards the environment around you will help you reconnect with the world around you. This will help you start enjoying life again.

Here are some of the strategies that can help you to stop living in your head and start living in the real world again.

Have Realistic Expectations

Sometimes we are plagued by negative thinking and overthinking simply because we have set expectations that far exceed our own abilities. When we set overly high standards for ourselves, we may end up getting disappointed when we fail to achieve them. Overthinking can lead to feelings of guilt, anger, anxiety, depression, and self-blame. In some cases, we may even aspire to do too much in a very limited amount of time. Not giving yourself enough time to accomplish a goal is self-sabotage. To avoid these problems you need to set attainable goals and give yourself enough time to accomplish them.

If you are prone to setting unrealistic expectations, it is important to re-evaluate your goals and assess whether they match your talents and skills. You should, therefore, give yourself ample time to plan your goals and draft a realistic plan of action. By doing so, you will be able to eliminate the tendency to overthink and develop a strong awareness of yourself and the environment around you.

Change Your Perspective

There are some instances where we struggle with overthinking simply because we hold a negative attitude towards a situation. When things do not go the way we expect, we may end up forming negative judgments about ourselves. To overcome this problem, you need to learn how to adjust your attitude towards the situation. Therefore, when a negative thought about a situation pops into your head, try to analyze whether there is something you can gain from the situation. In such cases, simply changing your attitude towards the situation can make a huge difference in how you handle it. It is important to let go of negative thoughts that do not help you in any way and replace them with productive thoughts that are designed to help you succeed. The more you practice superimposing positive thoughts over negative ones, the sooner you will turn this type of thinking into a habit. As a result, you will be able to approach even the most difficult situations with a dose of healthy optimism. This might even provide you with some fresh insights on how to solve the problem. Even if the situation is beyond your control, you might pick up some helpful lessons that may help you through a similar situation in the future.

Find a Good Distraction

When you are feeling overwhelmed with negative thoughts, sometimes it helps to find a good distraction to help you to release some of the tension and stress. There are times when all that is needed during a difficult moment of overthinking is to simply find something to help your mind calm down. When you find yourself overwhelmed with negative thinking, you can turn this energy into a creative distraction. For example, if you are artistically gifted, you can draw, paint, make crafts or play music. This will help you channel your energy in a productive way and distract your mind from the negative thought loops that you may be caught up in.

Even if you are not very creative, there are many things you can do to relax your mind when overthinking. For instance, you can read a book or watch a funny TV program to lift your mood.

Sometimes a good distraction can help you soothe anxiety resulting from negative thoughts.

Acknowledge that Some Things are Beyond your Control

No matter how much control you are able to exert over your life, there are plenty of things that are beyond your control. You cannot, for example, know whether you are going to have a bad day at work tomorrow. However, you can control how you react to the situations you face. Accepting that you cannot control everything in your life allows you to focus on changing things that you do have power over. This is a form of thinking that can help you overcome negative thoughts and the characteristic anxiety that comes with them.

Accept Your Limitations

As humans, we have a tendency to want to exert total control over our lives and our environment. This desire arises out of an evolutionary need for survival. However, the circumstances in the world aren't always in our control. While we have individual control over our lives to some extent, it is just not possible to know what will happen next in the unpredictable world that we live in. One minute you may be healthy and full of life, and the next minute you are diagnosed with a chronic illness, or you may be succeeding in a high paying career and then suddenly lose your job. Our inability to predict what happens in the world and our lives might seem very gloomy. However, this is a natural part of our reality and a fact that should be embraced. By acknowledging your limitations and lack of ability to control everything, you can ease the pressure on yourself and achieve a state of inner peace and acceptance. This will allow you to cope better with negative situations and prevent them from affecting your mental health.

You should always remember that overthinking is not a habit that yields any productive results. As a matter of fact, it only sinks you deeper into the hole of anxiety and despair. By accepting your limitations and focusing on what is realistic and achievable, you can more easily overcome negativity and appreciate all the wonderful things in your life.

Replace the Negative Thoughts

Acknowledging and releasing negative thoughts can help you generate opportunities for positive thoughts. Let's suppose that you have been fired from your job and are worried about how you are going to support your family. Rather than bombard yourself with negative thoughts such as "How will I survive without a job?", try to see any positive thing that you can derive from this situation. Consider thoughts such as "How can I capitalize on my free time?" By replacing your negative thoughts with positive ones, you may end up realizing the situation is not as gloomy as it seems. This can help you overcome the tendency to overthink and make room for positive, productive thoughts.

Talk Yourself Out of It

Overthinking often arises out of irrational fear or anxiety over certain situations. The recurrent mental chatter is usually not backed by any meaningful evidence based on reality. If you find yourself obsessing over negative thoughts, it might be helpful to interrogate yourself to find out why you are having negative thoughts. Having a logical conversation with yourself whenever you are overwhelmed with your negativity can help you determine whether those thoughts deserve to be paid any attention. In all likelihood, you will find that most of your worries are not very rational. This can help you ease your mind and stop overthinking too much.

Cultivate a Psychological Distance

One of the most effective ways of coping with negative thoughts and overthinking is to develop a psychological distance between them and yourself. As we mentioned in the previous chapter, your thoughts do not usually reflect reality. Likewise, they do not necessarily arise from you. As humans, we tend to view thoughts as things that are consciously being generated rather than images and words that occur autonomously. This causes us to identify with our thoughts too much.

However, the problem with getting too attached to our negative thoughts is that it makes us lose our sense of control when we are bombarded by them. Therefore, in order to prevent spiraling into patterns of negativity and overthinking, you need to learn how to detach yourself from your thoughts. Start using language in a way that treats thoughts as ideas that are happening separately from yourself. For instance, instead of thinking "I am a total failure," you can address your negative thought by saying, "I notice I am now having that thought which says I am a failure". By developing this kind of mindset, you will be able to cultivate a psychological distance between yourself and your negative thoughts so that they do not impact your mood or affect your peace of mind.

Practice Self Compassion

Self-compassion is a very effective way of dealing with difficult situations, including overthinking. It allows you to develop a deeper understanding of yourself, become more connected with others and increase your satisfaction in life.

By treating yourself with more compassion and understanding, you will realize that your happiness is entirely dependent on yourself. As a result, you will be able to navigate even the most difficult thoughts with confidence and optimism. This will help you eliminate the problem of negative thinking for good.

While overthinking is a very difficult problem to contend with, it should not give you a reason to despair. With the right strategies, you can empower yourself to deal with negative thoughts and overthinking in a positive way.

Summary

In this chapter, we learned how to stop overthinking. Here are the main things you need to remember when trying to overcome obsessive negative thoughts that do not help you move forward in any way.

- Practice self-observation to develop an awareness of your thoughts. This will help you gain mental clarity about them.
- Realize and understand the emotional triggers that cause you to overthink.
- Constantly remind yourself of your goals and aspirations.
- Realize and appreciate that overthinking is a problem that can be combated and eliminated successfully.
- Reconnect with other people and the outside world in order to stop living in your head and start living in the real world again.
- Learn how to replace your negative thoughts with positive ones.
- Develop a psychological distance between yourself and your thoughts to avoid becoming too identified with your negative thoughts.
- Learn to be more compassionate and kind to yourself and accept your limitations.
- Develop a stoic attitude towards life in order to become more resilient when faced with challenges.

If you have been struggling with overthinking, I assure you there is nothing wrong with you. Ruminating over negative thoughts is a problem that every individual experiences in their life (Oppong, 2020). However, by applying the strategies we have discussed in this chapter, you can develop the ability to get rid of your overthinking for good and have a more positive attitude.

In the next chapter, you will learn different techniques and practices that you can apply to cushion yourself from constant worrying, which is a side effect of overthinking.

CHAPTER SIX:

Overcoming Worry

Worrying is undoubtedly a very normal part of life. There are plenty of things that can cause you to worry. For instance, you may be apprehensive about getting to work late due to traffic gridlock or perhaps you worry that you will not be able to meet the deadline for your work project. These kinds of worries are very natural and pretty much everyone experiences them. However, when your worries become too many and unrelenting, this can be a cause for alarm.

Worrying too much not only saps your emotional and mental energy but can also be detrimental to your physical health (Robinson, 2020). People who worry constantly tend to suffer from numerous problems, including anxiety, depression, headaches, muscle tension, and poor concentration. When worry becomes too common in your life, it can even be debilitating, making it difficult for you to perform your duties and responsibilities. This can deprive you of peace of mind and sink you deeper into a hole of despair.

Incessant worry is a chronic problem that can be very difficult to deal with. You may find yourself constantly obsessing about every negative thought, leaving you no time to actually enjoy your life.

Notably, people who worry too much tend to hold both positive and negative ideas about worrying, which further intensifies the problem. For instance, some people believe that constant worrying might make them lose their sanity. Holding such negative beliefs about worry can compound the problem, and make it difficult for you to find permanent solutions.

Positive beliefs about worry can also be just as damaging and problematic as negative ones. In some cases, people believe that by worrying constantly, they will be able to steer clear of problems and trouble. Some even fall into the trap of thinking that worrying too much will help them find solutions to problems they are facing. This, however, couldn't be further from the truth. Worrying too much not only drains your energy and creativity but also distracts you from finding solutions to life's difficult situations. The stress hormones which are released when you worry too much can significantly take a toll on your health. Some of the problems associated with worry include:

- Increased headaches.
- Depression due to emotional fatigue.
- Increased production of stomach acid which leads to heartburn and ulcers.
- Increased hyperactivity of the brain which leads to stress.
- Breathing problems due to muscle tension.
- Weakened immune system.
- Rise in blood sugar which can lead to Type 2 diabetes.
- Increase in blood pressure which can lead to heart problems.
- Excess stress on the digestive system which can lead to gastrointestinal diseases.
- Low sex drive due to fatigue and loss of confidence.
- Irregular menstrual cycles due to hormonal imbalances caused by stress hormones.

Worrying is something that everyone does. However, when it becomes a constant habit, it can make you susceptible to all the problems mentioned above. In order to be able to tackle this problem, it is important to first establish whether you are just worrying about the normal stresses of life or are engaging in excessive worrying. Below, we outline some of the symptoms which will help you differentiate between normal worrying and excessive worrying.

Normal Worrying

- You take some few minutes before falling asleep to think about your upcoming challenges and tasks that you are meant to accomplish.
- People rarely describe you as a nervous or anxious person.
- You often notice a loss of appetite whenever you are anticipating a stressful event.
- Sometimes you find yourself needing to have a drink in order to relax your mind and body when experiencing a stressful situation.
- You often worry about things for short amounts of time and then move on from them after you rationalize them.

Excessive Worrying

- You find it difficult to fall asleep or get a good night's rest because you are overwhelmed with worrisome thoughts for which you have no immediate solution.
- People often describe you as very anxious and consider worrying to be a key part of your personality.
- You often experience significant weight changes due to binge eating or not eating at all when you are dealing with difficult situations.
- You tend to overanalyze every situation that you encounter regardless of how trivial or serious it is.
- You find yourself unable to enjoy your life because you are constantly ruminating over everything that happens.
- You find it difficult to go through your day without using drugs and alcohol as an escape from your worries.
- You always seem to be looking for something to be worried about. In other words, worrying is like an addiction that you cannot seem to get rid of.

While ending the cycle of constant worrying can admittedly be a very challenging thing to do, it is nonetheless very possible. There are some very effective techniques and strategies that you may employ to break out of your worrying loops.

Create a Daily Worry Period

As counterintuitive as it might seem, scheduling worry time is actually one of the most effective ways of dealing with worrying thoughts. Rather than avoiding your obsessive negative thoughts, this strategy requires you to allocate some time to ruminate over them. This strategy can be very beneficial in a number of ways. Firstly, by allocating some time to ruminate over your negative thoughts, you will be able to reach a state of acceptance, which can provide you with relief and help you tackle your situation in a calmer and more relaxed state of mind. In addition to this, creating a daily worry period teaches you to compartmentalize your worries in order to free up your mind to perform the rest of your day's tasks and responsibilities. Instead of wasting useful time ruminating over your thoughts throughout the day, this strategy enables you to deal with your worries at a convenient time, thereby ensuring you are able to carry out other important activities. When practiced consistently, the technique of designating "worry" time can significantly reduce your tendency to worry and lessen anxiety.

Here are some of the steps you need to follow in order to implement this strategy effectively:

1. Have a daily worry routine for a period of one week. Ideally, you should set your worry periods in the morning or during the day. Do not set your worry time at night right before going to bed, as it may interfere with your sleep.
2. During your allocated worry time, write down all the things that you are worried about. Refrain from trying to find solutions to all of your worries during this period. Writing down the worrisome thought in itself can be a huge source of relief, and

can provide you with a fresh perspective on how to tackle situations that you are worried about.

3. Train yourself to not worry in between your designated worry periods. If you find yourself having worrisome thoughts outside of your allocated worrying time, calmly remind yourself to shelve those thoughts until your next worry time. This can be a little hard to do at first, but with constant practice, it will soon become very easy to switch off your worries until your set worry period comes again.

4. At the end of your "worry" week, take some time to go over the notes that you wrote down during your daily worry periods. This will provide you with a lot of insights concerning your worry habits. For instance, you will notice whether you have any recurrent worries or some which are simply irrational.

5. Once you have completed your worry week, you can set a new one to determine the dynamics of your worrisome thoughts. With regular practice and consistency, you will begin to develop control over your worrisome thoughts and prevent them from interfering with your daily routines and your peace of mind.

Challenge Your Anxious Thoughts

Very often when we engage in constant worrying, it happens simply because we observe the world around us in a way that makes it seem overly cruel and frightening. For instance, we may tend to focus on the worst-case scenario in every situation or believe that our anxieties are reflective of reality. These types of mindsets are typically known as cognitive distortions since they make us perceive reality in an inaccurate way (Grohol, 2019). In order to overcome the problem of incessant worrying thoughts, it is important to become aware of the various types of cognitive distortions that create an untrue perception of reality. Here are 15 of the most common cognitive distortions which people experience:

1. Mental Filtering

This refers to a type of cognitive distortion whereby a person filters out all the positive aspects of a given situation and inflates the negative aspects, which they then focus all their attention on. For example, they may identify an unpleasant situation and focus on it to a point where it completely dominates their thinking.

2. Polarized Thinking

This is a form of thinking which only takes into account two opposing extremes of a particular idea, person or thing without factoring any nuances which may exist. It is also referred to as "black and white" thinking. Polarized thinking often fails to take into account the complexities and grey areas that characterize every individual or situation.

3. Overgeneralization

This is a cognitive distortion whereby an individual makes a conclusion about something, based entirely on very little evidence. This thinking pattern also fails to consider the nuances involved in different situations. So, a person who overgeneralizes might expect a negative situation to repeat itself simply because it happened once.

4. Jumping to Conclusions

An individual who jumps to conclusions assumes they always know what another person is thinking or feeling even without the other party expressing it outright. For instance, they may rush to conclude that someone is against them without bothering to verify whether it is actually true or not.

5. Catastrophizing

Catastrophizing (also known as magnifying) is a cognitive distortion whereby an individual expects the worst-case scenario in any kind of situation. People who engage in catastrophizing may inflate the importance of very insignificant events. For instance, they may believe that they will never be successful in their academic lives simply because they failed in one school test or exam.

6. Personalization

This is a type of cognitive distortion where an individual believes that everything other people say or do is a personal reaction towards them. People who personalize everything tend to feel attacked whenever someone mentions anything in a way that they do not agree with. They also tend to make comparisons between themselves and others in an effort to determine whether they are good enough or better than other people. Personalization is a key trigger for personal insecurity, anxiety, and low self-esteem.

7. Control Fallacies

Control fallacies involve two different, but closely related cognitive distortions. One form of control fallacy entails a belief that one's actions are controlled by external forces. For instance, an individual who engages in this type of cognitive distortion may believe that the reason why they are unable to perform well in school is because of their parent's divorce. On the flip side of this cognitive distortion is the internal control fallacy whereby an individual assumes responsibility for external events that they may not have anything to do with at all. For instance, they may believe that they are the reason why someone is hurt or angry when this is not the case at all. Both of these control fallacies can be very detrimental to one's mental wellness since they lead to overthinking, self-deprecation and self-blame.

8. Fallacy of Fairness

This is a cognitive distortion whereby a person thinks they know what is fair in every situation. So, when something happens contrary to their expectations, they are likely to judge it as unfair to themselves or others. Individuals who engage in this type of thinking are susceptible to feelings of resentment, anger, and helplessness. It is important to realize that life is not always fair, and things may not necessarily end up working out for someone even when they ought to.

9. Blaming

An individual who engages in blaming has a tendency of holding other people responsible for their suffering. In some cases, they may blame themselves for the emotional pain of others even when they have absolutely nothing to do with it. This usually exacerbates the problem of negative thinking and makes them constantly anxious. An individual who engages in this type of thinking ought to realize that nobody has power over our thoughts and emotions apart from ourselves.

10. "Should" Statements

As innocent as they might seem, "should" statements are actually a type of cognitive distortion that can contribute to worry and anxiety. This is because they create an impression of ironclad rules which you are expected to adhere to. Statements such as "I should work out to get the perfect body" or "I should be happy" exert undue pressure on you to act in a certain way in order to achieve certain expectations, which may not be realistic. When these statements are directed inwards, they often lead one to feel guilty or embarrassed in the event that they are unable to meet those expectations. On the other hand, when they are directed at others, they may cause us to be resentful or angry at them for not living up to the exceedingly high standards we have set for them.

11. Emotional Reasoning

This is a cognitive distortion whereby a person uses their emotions as evidence for an external reality or situation. Individuals who engage in emotional reasoning tend to make conclusions that whatever they are feeling is essentially true. Usually, this occurs when their emotions completely override their thinking. It is important to realize that while emotions are very powerful forces, they may not correctly reflect the reality of a particular situation.

12. Fallacy of Change

This is a cognitive distortion which arises out of one's expectation for people to change who they are in order to suit them. This is very common in relationships. A person may wrongly believe that if they pressure or cajole their partner enough, they might change who they are and turn into an idealized or perfect version of themselves.

13. Global Labelling

Global labeling can be thought of as an extreme kind of generalization. Typically, affected people tend to attach a negative universal label to themselves or others if they act in certain ways. For instance, if another person errs against them in any way, they may conclude that the person is a buffoon.

14. Always Being Right

There are some people who are under the impression that they are always right regardless of the situation. The affected people tend to be overly judgmental, and will continually put other people's opinions and actions on trial to prove that their own are absolutely right.

15. Heaven's Reward Fallacy

This is a type of cognitive distortion which is very similar to the fallacy of fairness. A person who falls victim to this kind of distortion wrongly believes that their sacrifices and self-denial will eventually pay off with some kind of grand reward. The problem with this fallacy is that it may lead to anger and resentment when the sacrifices that one makes do not get rewarded as they had hoped.

As you can see, there are plenty of cognitive distortions that can cloud our thinking and contribute to problems of worry and overthinking. In order to overcome worrisome thoughts, therefore, it is important to subject your thinking to scrutiny in order to determine whether it is backed by sound evidence or simply a result of deep-seated cognitive distortions (Grohol, 2019).

Know Which Worries are Solvable vs Unsolvable

Worrying is usually associated with feelings of anxiety and restlessness. However, there are some instances where worrying can actually reduce your anxiety. This is simply because ruminating makes you feel like you're actually working to come up with solutions for your situation. However, there is a huge difference between worrying and problem-solving. Worrying essentially doesn't provide any solutions because it approaches situations from a position of fear and anxiety. Problem-solving, on the other hand, takes into account facts and evidence when dealing with a problematic situation. Therefore, in order to overcome the problem of worrying too much, you need to distinguish between the worries that are solvable and those that are not.

A solvable worry is one for which there is a remedy or course of action that can be taken. For instance, if you are worried about not making it to an important office meeting due to traffic, you can call your supervisor or manager to inform them about it beforehand. An unsolvable worry, on the other hand, is one that doesn't have an immediate course of action. For example, worrying about getting sick in the future.

Once you have identified worries that are solvable, you need to start brainstorming on the possible solutions to the problem you are facing. As you do so, try to focus on the things that you can control and make a comprehensive plan of action on how to execute them. If you determine that your worries are not solvable, try and accept the uncertainty about the future, and focus your energies on living in the present. Constantly worrying about the future can distract you from enjoying and appreciating the gifts and privileges that you currently have.

Avoid Getting Caught up in Vague Fears

Very often when we experience vague fears which are not fully understood, we tend to get caught up in them, which leads to worrying and anxiety. This happens because we focus on the worst-case outcome of the situation that we are facing. This, however, is very counterproductive, and only leads to more anxiety and a relentless cycle of unresolvable worrisome thoughts. In order to overcome this tendency to worry over vague fears, it is important for you to investigate them and determine whether such worries are valid or only the result of mental chatter. You can approach this situation by asking yourself, "What is the worst possible outcome that this situation may lead to?" Once you have answered that question to the best of your understanding, try to brainstorm some of the ways in which you can respond to the situation in case those fears materialize. You may end up realizing that the worst-case scenario of the particular situation is not nearly as bad as you imagined. By cross-examining your fears in this manner, therefore, you will be able to get rid of the tendency to worry about fears that are irrational and become more adept at managing your unsolvable worries.

Interrupt the Worry Cycle

If you find that you worry too much, it can be easy to assume that you are doomed to have worrisome thoughts forever. However, there are several simple strategies that you can employ to interrupt your worrying loops and achieve peace of mind. These include exercise and yoga.

Exercise

As we discussed previously, regular exercise can help disrupt your worrisome thoughts, fight stress and reduce anxiety. This is in addition to keeping your body in a healthy condition and enhancing your overall well being. Don't forget, even a little exercise, such as a brisk walk, or going up a flight of stairs will help.

Yoga

The practice of yoga can be very beneficial when it comes to dealing with worrying thoughts. There are various types of yoga, all of which are meant to improve various aspects of our lives. Some of the benefits of yoga include improved blood circulation, an increase in energy and vitality, better cognition and improved flexibility.

Yoga has also been proven to increase the overall health and wellness of people. Practitioners of yoga tend to manifest greater satisfaction in their lives and are less anxious or depressed than those who do not. This is not surprising, considering the fact that all schools of yoga teach and emphasize the need for people to become more aware of the present and live in it. By learning and practicing yoga you can cope with the daily worries of life more effectively and prevent them from interfering with your health and wellness.

Meditation

Meditation is one of the most powerful ways of coping with worry and anxiety. This practice is founded upon the premise that worrying about the past or the future takes one out of the present and leads to anxiety and unhappiness. Meditation is meant to help us live in the present by making us aware of what is happening around us in the moment. People who practice meditation enjoy better health and higher levels of contentment compared to those who do not. By practicing meditation and mindfulness you can disrupt your worrisome thoughts and increase your awareness not only of yourself but of the world around you.

Summary

In this chapter, you have learned about how to overcome the cycle of worry. We have discussed how worrisome thoughts arise, what contributes to them and how we can cope with them in a healthy manner. To recap the main ideas discussed in this chapter, here are the techniques and practices you need to observe in order to get rid of your worries for good:

- Set aside a "worry" period in order to investigate your worrisome thoughts and prevent them from interfering with your productivity.

- Challenge your worrisome thoughts to determine whether they have any validity or are simply the automatic thinking patterns arising from cognitive distortions.
- Become aware of the worries that are solvable and those that are not solvable in order to redirect your energies in a productive way that is geared towards problem-solving, rather than ruminating.
- Disrupt your worry cycles by performing exercises, practicing yoga and meditation.

In the next chapter, we are going to explore the idea of positive thinking and how you can cultivate it to deal with negative thoughts. We will explore some of the ways of identifying negative thinking and the benefits you can derive from thinking positively.

CHAPTER SEVEN:

Being More Positive to Reduce Stress

The power of positive thinking has been a point of discussion for many psychologists and wellness experts. While some people scoff at the benefits of positive thinking, there are many advocates of this practice who consider it a very useful tool for approaching life's challenging situations. If you have been struggling with negative thoughts and worry, applying positive thinking can help you overcome these problems and reclaim your power over your thoughts. So in this chapter, we are going to look at how you can develop a positive attitude in order to reduce stress and anxiety.

What is Positive Thinking?

Well, when most people think about the idea of positive thinking, the impressions that come to mind are those of blissful ignorance in the face of difficult situations. However, this couldn't be further from the truth. Positive thinking does not mean burying your head in the sand and ignoring any difficult situations that you may be faced with. On the contrary, positive thinking is a mindset that approaches challenges with a sense of optimism and confidence. Individuals who are positive thinkers tend to focus on the brighter side of things, even when they meet challenges on the way ("Positive thinking: Stop negative self-talk to reduce stress," 2020a)

Positive thinking is very effective when it comes to alleviating the stress and anxiety that comes with negative thoughts and overthinking. To understand why developing a positive mindset is important, let us briefly look at how positive thinking works.

Positive Thinking and Self Talk

The aim of positive thinking is not to ignore the problems and challenging situations you encounter in life. As a matter of fact, a positive mindset simply refers to the practice of approaching a difficult situation with a winning attitude. So, instead of focusing on the worst-case scenario in any given situation, you pay attention to the proverbial silver lining.

The genesis of any positive mindset is typically the "self-talk", which refers to the stream of thoughts that are constantly running through our minds. These thoughts often stem from logic and reason, although they may also come from our fears, beliefs, and habits that we may have cultivated over the course of our lives. If your stream of thoughts is mostly negative, then you are likely to develop a pessimistic worldview and mindset. On the other hand, if your automatic thoughts are generally positive, you most likely perceive the world through an optimistic state of mind. Developing a positive mindset is not always easy, given the numerous unpleasant situations we often find ourselves in. In essence, it might be very difficult to focus on the brighter side of life when things aren't going the way you hoped. However, there are plenty of benefits that you can enjoy from being a positive thinker, which makes the whole endeavor very worthwhile.

Benefits of Positive Thinking

Here are some of the benefits that you can enjoy from developing a positive mindset and learning to think positively.

Reduced Stress

Positive thinking has been proven to have amazing stress reduction properties. People who practice positive thinking are less likely to suffer from stress and depression. This has to do with the fact that positive thinkers tend to focus their energies on solving an unpleasant situation rather than wallowing in self-pity and helplessness. They are, therefore, able to troubleshoot their stressors faster and more effectively.

Increased Life Span

Research has shown that individuals with a positive mindset tend to live longer than those who constantly think negatively. This is because negative thoughts and emotions usually have a detrimental effect on our health. When they are eliminated, therefore, the physical implications on the body are also reversed, thereby allowing one to enjoy better health.

Better Cognition

Constant negative thinking and overthinking usually impact our cognitive abilities in a negative way. A pessimistic mindset can seriously interfere with your concentration and recall ability. By developing a positive mindset, however, you ease mental and psychological pressure, improve your mental clarity and optimize your cognitive function.

Improved Relationships

Positive thinkers tend to be more open, compassionate and fun to be around. This makes them highly attractive. Therefore, by getting rid of your negative thinking habits, you may become more connected with people and improve the quality of your relationships with your family, friends, and workmates.

Increased Success

Positive people are generally more likely to succeed in their careers as well as personal lives. This is because they tend to see and pursue more opportunities in life compared to their pessimistic counterparts.

Positive-minded individuals are also less likely to focus on their failures, as this helps them avoid getting discouraged when things don't go according to plan.

Better Cardiovascular Health

Individuals who practice positive thinking are less likely to suffer from cardiovascular illnesses such as hypertension and stroke. This is because they are able to deal with stress and anxiety in productive ways and prevent them from interfering with their health and personal development.

As you can see, there are numerous advantages that you can enjoy by shifting your perspective and thinking more positively. Apart from safeguarding your health and improving your overall quality of life, thinking positively can greatly empower you to achieve all your goals and aspirations in life. If you have been grappling with negative thoughts and overthinking, developing a positive mindset can provide you with relief from anxiety and stress and enable you to cope better with unpleasant situations. ("Positive thinking: Stop negative self-talk to reduce stress," 2020a)

Perform Random Acts of Kindness

When we get too caught up in our worries and negative thoughts, we become too absorbed in them that we forget other people are facing challenges very similar to our own. To cultivate positive mindedness, it is vital to take the time from our lives and perform acts of kindness towards other people. If you are dealing with negative thoughts and worries, consider stepping outside your daily routine and do something for someone else for a change. This can be as simple as complimenting a random stranger or helping out a friend with a task which they are working on. Performing acts of kindness for other people will help you reconnect with the real world and regain perspective on your own life. This can help you become a more positive-minded person and provide you with opportunities to share your unique talents and gifts with others.

Learn to Accept Criticism in a Positive Way

Human beings, in general, have a strong aversion towards criticism. This is because we tend to take criticism very personally. Whenever someone mentions something critical about us, our minds immediately begin to come up with negative judgments about our character and causes us to become defensive. This makes it very difficult for us to accept criticism in a graceful manner even when it is valid and well-intentioned. However, to become positive-minded people, we need to change this mindset and become more open to criticism.

Very often when we are criticized, we tend to think that there is a fundamental flaw in ourselves that is being exposed for all to see. This can lead to problems such as anxiety and overthinking as we struggle to justify whether or not the criticism was warranted. It is important to realize that criticism of our thoughts or actions is not fundamentally an attack on our character. Therefore, we need to learn how to divorce the two from each other.

When you receive any kind of criticism, instead of reacting to it in a knee-jerk kind of way, take a moment to internalize the criticism and give it some thought. This will prevent you from falling victim to rash reactions such as lashing out at the other person. That reaction might then lead to an escalation or volatile disagreement. Once you have taken the time to mentally digest the criticism, try to look for any positive lessons or points which you can derive from it. Of course, not all criticism will be conveyed politely. The person criticizing you might be unnecessarily brash or insensitive in the way they present their opinion. However, even if they are rude, try to see the positive aspects which you can derive from their criticism. Once you begin to see the criticism in a positive light, thank the other person for their words. They might have presented their criticism in a rude way simply because they are having a bad day. So refrain from the temptation of judging them too harshly. If you realize that the criticism was accurate, make a conscious effort to learn from it since this will help you become a better person.

Summary

This chapter has introduced the concept and benefits of positive thinking. We have looked at the ways in which learning how to evaluate your negative thinking loops can help you change your mindset from a pessimistic worldview to one which sees and focuses on the brighter side of things. In conclusion, here are the big takeaways from this chapter:

- Positive thinking is not the practice of avoiding or ignoring difficult situations, rather, it involves approaching difficult situations with an attitude of optimism and problem solving.
- Developing a positive mindset can be very beneficial in a number of ways including stress reduction, enhanced cognition, and improved overall health.
- In order to achieve a positive mindset, it is crucial to learn how to avoid automatic negative thinking pitfalls that we get caught up in. These include polarizing, labeling, catastrophizing and personalizing.
- One of the best things that you can do to get away from your own negativity is to perform random acts of kindness.

Nevertheless, shifting your mindset from a negative to a positive one is not a simple matter. It requires immense willpower, practice, and dedication. In all likelihood, you will struggle to achieve this during the initial stages of your practice. However, with the right tools and techniques, you will certainly develop a positive mindset that will help you overcome the tendency to worry too much or obsess over negative thoughts.

In the following chapter, we are going to look at how you can cultivate the practice of positive thinking. Some of the topics we will discuss include how to identify areas in your thinking that need improvement, and how a healthy lifestyle can help you develop a positive mindset. By the end of the chapter, you should be fully equipped with the knowhow and skills to navigate any negative thought patterns that you typically experience.

CHAPTER EIGHT:

Cultivating Positive Thinking

In the previous chapter, we looked at how your mindset can impact your life. You will no doubt agree, then, that developing a positive mindset can help you get rid of your tendency to worry and allow you to live a happier and more productive life. As a matter of fact, how we perceive the world and interact with it is to a large extent dependent on our mindset. That is why it is always important to remain positive about every aspect of life. Be that as it may, changing your mindset is not something that happens magically overnight.

Developing positive thinking is a process that takes a lot of time and mental investment to accomplish. This, however, does not mean that you need to be a special kind of person to achieve this. Anyone can cultivate a positive mindset, provided they are committed to changing the way they think and have the right strategies to help them (Hurst, 2014).

In this chapter, we are going to explore some of the useful techniques and methods you can apply when cultivating positive thinking. These highly effective strategies will allow you to orchestrate a paradigm shift in the way you think, and empower yourself to get rid of negative thinking.

Focus on Positive Thinking

Cultivating a positive mindset requires you to redirect your attention from the negative thoughts that you are constantly plagued by, and focus on the positive thoughts about any particular situation. A common example is this perspective is a person's answer to the question "Is the glass half empty or half full?" A positive person will say it is half full. This is easier said than done, considering the fact that we are often inclined to obsess over negative thoughts and downplay any good that may be present. Nevertheless, just as you can develop a bad habit of focusing on negativity, you can likewise reverse this and learn how to think positively.

Identify Areas to Change

The first thing you need to do when learning how to be a more positive-minded individual is to identify areas in your life that need to be changed. Perhaps your negative thought patterns stem from dissatisfaction with your career or an unhealthy relationship. By figuring out the situations that contribute to your negative thinking, you will be able to begin changing this aspect of your life and get rid of the problem. For instance, if negative thoughts arise because you feel unfulfilled at work, you may address this issue with your boss to come up with ways to make the situation more satisfying for you. Likewise, if you are unhappy with your relationship, you can have a mature discussion with your partner to see how you can improve it and make it more fulfilling. Remember, the goal of identifying your triggers for negative thinking and overthinking is to come up with workable solutions to whatever issues you are facing to get rid of the problem of ruminating.

Check Yourself

For you to develop a positive mindset and get rid of the tendency to overthink, you need to become aware of the thoughts that constantly run through your mind during the course of the day. This is a strategy known as "checking yourself". The aim of this practice is to find out whether you experience more negative thoughts than positive ones. If you realize that most of the thoughts you experience as you go about your day are negative, you need to try and find a way of replacing them with positive thoughts about the same situations.

Be Open to Humor

Having a good laugh undoubtedly has plenty of benefits, which can hardly be overstated. Some of the health benefits of laughter include enhanced blood circulation in the body, the release of muscle tension and triggering of the release of endorphins like serotonin and dopamine, which make us feel good and content. Humor also provides stress relief and can help you get rid of the anxiety you commonly experience when plagued with negative thinking. Poking fun at yourself also helps you perceive life less seriously, and can relieve you of the constant pressures and worries of life, which make you think negatively. By being open to humor, you may come to the realization that some of the problems that you constantly obsess over are not nearly as big as you think. Consequently, this will enable you to develop a better mindset and approach the challenges you encounter in life with a positive attitude.

Adopt and Practice a Healthy Lifestyle

When it comes to developing a positive mindset, maintaining a healthy lifestyle is absolutely vital. This is because the more you take care of your body, the faster you can reverse the physical and mental toll that stressful thoughts and anxiety exact from you. Therefore, you need to adopt and maintain a daily exercise regime to stay fit and improve your overall health and wellness. Set aside some time, ideally 20-40 minutes, 2-3 days per week to perform some physical exercise such as jogging, walking, dancing or stretching. By sticking to good workout habits, you will not only improve your physical health but also your mental state.

In addition to exercise, it is also vital to adopt a healthy diet in order to promote a positive mindset. There are plenty of foods that are known to increase anxiety, and should, therefore, be avoided if you are trying to get rid of negative thinking. These include processed foods, soft drinks, coffee, refined sugars, and dairy. You should also minimize or cut out alcohol completely when trying to cultivate a positive mindset. Some of the foods you can opt for instead include asparagus, almonds, avocado, nuts, kales, and spinach.

By maintaining a regular workout regime and eating healthy, you can build up your physical and mental resilience, which will help you overcome negative thinking patterns and develop a more positive outlook on life.

Surround Yourself with Positive People

Having positive people around you can significantly improve your mindset, and help you become a more positive thinking individual. You need to ensure that the people you spend time with are supportive of you as a person and accept your personality with all the quirks and nuances it comes with. There are several reasons why surrounding yourself with positive-minded people is one of the best things you can do when forging a positive mindset.

It Promotes Authenticity

Positive minded friends and relatives typically desire to see you become the best version of yourself. Therefore, they will support you in your aspirations and goals. They will accept your personal decisions and the manner in which you express yourself. Having positive minded individuals around you will encourage you to embrace yourself. This means you won't need to walk on eggshells to avoid offending them or work too hard to impress them. This can take off a significant amount of mental pressure and make you feel more at ease.

Less Drama in Your Life

Positive-minded people tend to have a very low tolerance for unnecessary drama. They prefer to steer clear of negative energy and focus on being the best version of themselves and connecting with others. By seeking out positive people, therefore, you can avoid meaningless drama, which serves no purpose other than to increase stress, tension, and frustration. In doing so, you will be able to get rid of anxiety and enjoy greater peace of mind.

Provides you With Motivation

Having positive-minded people in your life can also increase your motivation significantly. Positive minded individuals tend to challenge themselves to do or be better. They focus all their energies on building themselves and others up. Having these kinds of people around can provide you with enough motivation to make positive changes in your life and become a better person.

Take Up a New Hobby

Adopting a new hobby can seem like a very challenging task, given the fact that you will have to learn everything from scratch. If you are a career person with very little free time, or constantly busy with family obligations, it can seem impossible to fit your new interest into your already packed schedule. However, starting a new hobby can actually be very beneficial when it comes to cultivating a positive mindset. Taking up a new hobby not only allows you to learn and develop new skills but also allows you to explore your personality more. You might be surprised to discover that you have some latent talents and abilities which you never knew you had. So, when working on improving your positive thinking, try to select a hobby that you are interested in. This can be something like birdwatching, painting, playing a musical instrument, gardening or anything else you feel like you have always wanted to do. Starting a new hobby will enable you to connect with yourself and enjoy a new measure of fulfillment.

Practice Positive Self Talk

Self-talk refers to the internal monologue that is always taking place in your head even as you go about the ordinary activities of your day-to-day life (Holland, 2019). This is usually reflective of your core values, belief-systems, and ideas. Self-talk can be either positive or negative, depending on your personality and experiences. Therefore, if you are a naturally optimistic person, you will likely have positive thoughts and self-talk. On the other hand, if you are a pessimist, your self-talk will mostly be negative. In order to cultivate a positive mindset, you need to shift this internal monologue from negative thoughts to positive ones.

There are plenty of benefits that you can derive from practicing positive self-talk. These include:

- Greater satisfaction with life.
- Improved immune system.
- Better cardiovascular health.
- Stress and anxiety relief.
- Longer lifespan.

When practicing positive self-talk, the key is to identify any negative thoughts that you might be having and replace them with a positive outlook. For instance, instead of saying "I am a failure and will never be good at anything" you can replace that thought by saying "I'm glad I tried my best, I will try to do better next time." By using compassionate words when addressing your negative self-talk, you will be able to get yourself out of the trap of negative thinking and become more accepting of yourself and the situations that are beyond your control ("Positive thinking: Stop negative self-talk to reduce stress," 2020b).

Learn to Laugh at Yourself

As human beings, we tend to be very critical of ourselves. We constantly gauge ourselves against the achievements of other people and set exceedingly high standards for ourselves. When we fail to meet these standards, we may end up being disappointed in ourselves. This disappointment often gives rise to negative feelings of unworthiness and self-blame which can significantly damage our self-esteem. It is important to realize that nobody is perfect, including the people we look up to and who seem to be good at everything. Therefore, we need to get rid of the tendency to expect perfection from ourselves. Learning to laugh at ourselves and our mistakes can help ease the pressure of performing and allow us to become more positive about our lives. It is vital to remember that life is essentially an adventure and that all of us are on the path of self-discovery. Adopting a lighthearted attitude towards our flaws and idiosyncrasies, therefore, will allow us to approach life with perpetual optimism and provide us with a greater appreciation of our lives.

Summary

In this chapter you learned about positive thinking and how to develop this mindset. We have discussed how positive thinking can improve your mindset and enhance your overall health and wellbeing. Granted, this is not something that happens instantaneously. You will need to practice these techniques over a period of time to begin seeing tangible results. However, there is no denying that these tips and techniques will work for you just as they have worked for a lot of people in the past.

To recap the main points of this chapter, here are some of the tips you need to remember when cultivating a positive mindset:

- Developing positive thinking does not happen overnight - it requires diligence and practice.
- Learn how to observe your thoughts consciously to recognize the negative thoughts that you tend to ruminate over most frequently. This will help you to determine which situations trigger negative thinking patterns in you, and how you can

change those situations in order to become more positive minded.

- Embrace humor and learn to laugh at yourself and the situations you find yourself in. Taking your life less seriously will reduce the pressure you experience when faced with difficult situations.

- Adopt and maintain a healthy lifestyle which includes regular physical exercises and a healthy diet. This will not only keep your body in good shape but will also provide you with relief from anxiety and stress.

- Surround yourself with positive-minded people who will motivate and encourage you to be the best version of yourself. Find friends who are accepting of the person you are and who constantly challenge you to become the person that you aspire to be.

- Practice positive self-talk by replacing negative thoughts and phrases you may be prone to with positive ones. Always focus on the brighter side of things even when dealing with difficult situations. This will prevent you from falling into the traps of negative thinking cycles, and allow you to be more proactive in finding solutions to the immediate problems you face.

Positive thinking is a concept that goes hand in hand with self-acceptance. As a matter of fact, the practice of positive thinking typically leads to a better understanding of ourselves and allows us to realize and appreciate both our strengths and weaknesses as individuals. Just as it is important to cultivate positive thinking, it is also equally vital to learn how to accept who we are.

In the next chapter, we are going to explore the concept of self-acceptance, why it is crucial when it comes to dealing with negative thoughts, and some of the ways in which you can cultivate a greater acceptance of yourself. I have no doubt in my mind that at the end of the chapter, you will have a greater understanding of self-acceptance and why it is so vital when it comes to combating problems of overthinking, worry and anxiety.

CHAPTER NINE:

The Path to Self Acceptance

Many people confuse self-esteem with self-acceptance. While self-esteem refers to how you see yourself, self-acceptance refers to the feeling of satisfaction you have about yourself regardless of past mistakes and flaws.

How we perceive ourselves is very important to our psychological health as well as to our progress towards our goals and aspirations. People who display high self-worth tend to be highly driven, and they can pursue their goals regardless of the challenges they encounter along the way. On the other hand, people who have a poor sense of self-worth tend to get discouraged easily and are not as resilient when it comes to chasing their ultimate goals in life. They may avoid challenging situations, or find it difficult to persevere when they encounter stressful situations in life (F, 2008).

Individuals who have a poor sense of self-worth tend to perceive themselves negatively and are prone to problems such as anxiety, low self-esteem and a lack of self-confidence. Consequently, they tend to be less successful than their counterparts who have a high sense of self-worth.

In order to truly gain a sense of self-acceptance, it is absolutely vital to accept yourself fully, both the negative as well as the positive aspects of yourself. However, most people find it hard to admit their flaws to themselves, and even once they do, they may still find it difficult to live with these flaws. This often leads to feelings of insecurity, anxiety, and worry which can interfere not only with one's mental health but also hinder them from pursuing the goals that they have set out to achieve in their lives.

Benefits of Self Acceptance

Nevertheless, as difficult as it may be to achieve a sense of self-acceptance, doing so can be very rewarding in a number of ways. Here are some of the benefits that you can enjoy from learning how to accept yourself.

Allows You to Develop Humility

Practicing self-acceptance can help you become a more humble individual. The art of self-acceptance prompts us to acknowledge that we are not in total control of our reality and the world. With a balanced sense of self-acceptance, therefore, you are able to come to the realization that you are simply one piece of a much bigger puzzle known as life. Arriving at this realization allows you to become a more balanced and humble individual.

Enables You to Have a Clear Perspective on Reality

The art of self-acceptance enables you to have an awareness of a reality that is grounded in truth rather than fantasy. By practicing self-acceptance, you can see the world as it is rather than how you wish it would be. This can be very useful in helping you ground yourself and approach situations from a realistic point of view.

Helps You Become Better at Solving Problems

Self-acceptance gives you clarity of thought which you require to thoroughly evaluate your prevailing predicaments and find effective solutions to your most critical issues. When you are realistic about yourself and your abilities, you are more likely to plan and take a path that is likely to have a successful outcome.

Promotes Your Physical, Mental and Emotional Wellbeing

Living in denial about who we are can significantly interfere with the equilibrium of our lives due to the stress and anxiety that come with it. However, when we fully accept ourselves, we end up with increased energy to channel into more productive activities. This helps catapult us towards our life's goals and aspirations.

Improves Your Relationships with Others

Practicing self-acceptance can help us improve how we relate to the people around us. This is because it trains us to be more assertive with our needs, while also acknowledging that other people are different from us and may not share the same beliefs or values that we have. By learning how to accept ourselves, we can connect with people in much more meaningful ways and build relationships that are based on trust, honesty and mutual respect.

Provides You with an Option When Faced with Difficult Situations

Early on in the course of this book, we discussed the importance of being able to distinguish between solvable and unsolvable worries. Solvable worries are essentially those situations where immediate action can or has to be taken. Unsolvable worries are those that are essentially beyond your control. When we engage in ruminating or overthinking, it is often because we are faced with challenging situations for which we do not have an immediate solution. This can lead to feelings of hopelessness, helplessness, and anxiety. Self-acceptance, however, can help us cope better with these challenges. By accepting things that you do not have control over, you can relieve your mind from unproductive thoughts that serve no purpose other than to increase your anxiety and stress.

Enables You to Develop a Better Understanding of Yourself

Our emotions and feelings usually provide us with a lot of information about the things that we value in life. When you suppress or deny your emotions, you can end up feeling alienated from the world and lose sight of who you are. However, by acknowledging and accepting your feelings, you can develop a better understanding of yourself and be able to make decisions that align with your core values and beliefs.

Eliminates the Chances of Uncomfortable Feelings Coming Up Later

Developing an awareness of your feelings and emotions is an essential part of self-acceptance. When you acknowledge your uncomfortable emotions without suppressing or denying them, you are able to resolve them conclusively and promptly, so that they do not emerge later to haunt you.

Allows You to Forgive Yourself

Granted, all of us have done some things in the past, which we are not especially proud of. We may have made some gross errors or mistakes that have impacted our lives in significant ways. Obviously, the past cannot be undone, however, by acknowledging your flaws and past mistakes through self-acceptance, you can forgive yourself for past transgressions and move forward in life honestly and peacefully.

Frees You From the Tendency to Overthink

Very often, we get caught up in loops of overthinking and overanalyzing, simply because we are unable to accept the way things are at present, or we worry about the future, or we can't stop replaying the past in our heads. By practicing self-acceptance, however, we can overthink situations less, thereby conserving our energy and safeguarding our peace of mind.

Allows You to Attain Inner Peace

When you let go of your tendency to idealize, regret or worry about your past or future, you become more in tune with the real world. By accepting yourself for who you are, therefore, you can begin to appreciate the ordinary things in your life a lot more. This will consequently make you more comfortable in who you are and enable you to achieve inner peace and tranquility, even in the face of challenging situations.

A Way of Showing Gratitude to Yourself

Constantly engaging in negative thinking and overthinking can make you very self-critical and overly judgmental of yourself and your actions. This often promotes a victim mentality in us, where we perceive ourselves as less than we are. Practicing self-acceptance, however, allows us to become more compassionate and grateful for ourselves, which can help us become happier and more comfortable with ourselves.

Make You Psychologically Stronger

Whenever we try to avoid the aspects of ourselves that we are ashamed or unapproving of, we gradually lose our confidence and courage. This can be very detrimental to our psychological well being. By accepting yourself wholly, however, you will be able to face your fears and anxieties head-on, thus developing your psychological resilience.

Allows You to Assert Control Over Your Life

The practice of self-acceptance can help you to take control of your thoughts and actions. Whenever you accept a situation that seems very difficult or uncomfortable, you redirect your focus to what you need to do and take actions that are in alignment with your personal values and core beliefs.

Allows You to Discover Your Inherent Gifts and Talents

Practicing self-acceptance can help you to uncover all the talents and gifts that you may have kept under the surface. By recognizing the good in yourself and capitalizing on your assets, you will be able to accomplish new things! The ability to accept yourself fully brings to the forefront all of the parts of you which you have hidden from yourself and others all along. You will be surprised at how impactful these concealed gifts can be, not only to you personally but to other people as well.

How to Practice Self Acceptance

Self-acceptance is typically very challenging for people due to the fact that they constantly engage in self-doubt and self-criticism. The more these doubts and negative thoughts press upon their conscious awareness, the less confident they feel. This can lead to feelings of self-loathing and depression. If you struggle with the problem of poor self-worth, it is absolutely vital for you to nurture in yourself healthy self-acceptance. In order to do so, you must perceive self-acceptance as a skill that you can develop with practice, rather than an innate trait that only exists in a special class of people.

There are several techniques that can help you to develop a sense of self-acceptance and self-worth. Some of these techniques are listed below.

Practice Relaxed Awareness

To develop a strong sense of self-awareness, it is crucial to become aware of your thoughts and emotions. This is easier than you might think. Rather than trying really hard to focus your concentration on specific thoughts, you want to practice relaxed awareness. This refers to a state of awareness of your thoughts and emotions that you achieve when you let go of your preoccupation with attending to specific items or topics. Relaxed awareness can be compared to meditation, in the sense that it allows you to go about your life in an ordinary and normal manner, while operating at a higher level of awareness than most people usually do.

Here is a brief guide on how you can cultivate a state of relaxed awareness and reap the numerous benefits that this state of mind provides:

- Become mindful of your day-to-day actions such as showering, preparing your meals, brushing your teeth, etc. while being relaxed. Avoid trying to focus too much as you do this. Instead, maintain a calm and relaxed state of mind and be present in the moment.

- Acknowledge your uniqueness and develop an appreciation of what you have to offer yourself, the people you know, and the community you live in.
- Try to live in the present and shed off any worries or desires you may have about the past or the future. Focus on what you can actually do or are doing in the short term.
- See each day as a fresh opportunity to learn something new, and bring all your talents and gifts to whatever you do.

Acknowledge What You Notice

When you begin to practice relaxed awareness, you may notice many thoughts, emotions, and feelings running through your mind and body. These include self-deprecating thoughts and fears, as well as pleasant emotions such as contentment and joy. Naturally, you may be inclined to try and suppress some of the thoughts and feelings which you perceive as negative. However, this is counterproductive to your practice of self-acceptance, since these perceived negative thoughts and emotions are an inextricable part of yourself. Instead of trying to avoid them, acknowledge and welcome these negative thoughts just as you do the positive ones. Remember that these negative thoughts present you with an opportunity to learn something about yourself. Just don't dwell on them! This will lead you to a better understanding of your highly complex personality, and allow you to achieve self-acceptance.

Stop Comparing Yourself to Others

As human beings, we have a natural tendency to compare ourselves with other people. We tend to compare the best features of others against the average ones in ourselves. We often rank ourselves using imaginary scorecards. When we perceive ourselves as faring better than others, we feel a sense of validation. On the other hand, when we think that other people are better than us, this can lead to self-esteem and self-confidence issues.

As natural and harmless as it might seem, comparing ourselves to others is actually a very harmful habit that can wreak havoc on our lives and emotional health if not kept in check (Raftlova, 2019). To achieve self-acceptance, it is essential to let go of this habit. This is not always easy to do, considering how entrenched this habit usually is. In most cases, we make these comparisons subconsciously without even being aware of it.

However, by practicing relaxed awareness, you will begin to notice how you get caught up in comparing yourself to others. If you become aware of these thoughts, do not try to suppress or avoid them. Instead, acknowledge them and then let go of them by shifting your focus from them to positive thoughts.

Practice Gratitude

Acknowledging the things you are grateful for in life will make you more appreciative of your situation. It will also give you the energy to face life with a renewed sense of optimism and acceptance. When we focus on the good things we have in our lives, we have no time or space in our minds for negativity.

Learn to Forgive Yourself

Very often, we get caught up in negative thinking loops due to constant self-judgment and self-blame. Forgiving yourself is one of the hardest things to do. Granted, we may have made many mistakes in the past which continue to cast a dark cloud over our lives. However, constantly obsessing over past errors only keeps us stuck in negativity, and hinders our ability to move forward with our lives. Therefore, in order to foster healthy self-acceptance, it is very vital to forgive yourself and let go of the shame, guilt or sorrow of past mistakes.

Cultivating Self Compassion

Becoming more compassionate with yourself is a fundamental step towards achieving self-acceptance and inner peace. Many times, we get stuck in patterns of thinking which involve self-blame and unwarranted self-criticism. This can cause us to have a poor sense of self-worth and rob us of happiness and contentment.

However, by cultivating self-compassion, we can overcome the tendency to beat ourselves down, and we can become more accepting of ourselves. Here are some of the ways in which you can practice self-compassion and attain a balanced state of self-acceptance.

Change Your Mindset

Very often, we experience a poor sense of self-worth because we judge ourselves based on mistakes we may have done in the past. This can be detrimental to our self-esteem and confidence. To heal from past traumas and mistakes, you need to learn to separate your past actions from your current self and realize that your actions in the past do not have to have any bearing on the person you are now unless you want them to.

Spend Time Doing Things That You Love

When you are struggling with feelings of guilt and shame, it is easy to think that you don't deserve anything good in life. However, this couldn't be further from the truth. All of us, regardless of our past actions and mistakes, deserve happiness and fulfillment. Therefore, despite any transgressions of your past, you need to allow yourself to experience happiness by taking time to do things that you love, such as hobbies and interests. This show of self-love will help you to heal and develop a greater appreciation for yourself.

Avoid Making Judgments and Assumptions about Yourself

When you are grappling with negative thoughts about yourself, it is very easy to make blanket judgments and assumptions about your character. For instance, you may think that you are a failure, a bad person or unworthy of love. In doing so, you merely write yourself off and limit your options in terms of what you can do in the future. This is an incorrect mindset, and can significantly hinder you from making progress in life. Therefore, it is important to avoid judging yourself too harshly for your actions, and especially any mistakes in your past. Doing so will help you to acknowledge your actions and move closer to attaining a state of self-acceptance.

Be Mindful

The practice of mindfulness is very useful when it comes to self-compassion. Mindfulness allows you to be in the present moment and enables you to be consciously aware of your thoughts and emotions. By bringing your feelings and thoughts to the forefront of your conscious attention, you can learn to appreciate them and develop an acceptance of yourself.

Try Something New in Life

If you are like most people, you probably have a set of routines that you perform on a daily basis. Routines are very important because they give our lives a sense of stability and comfort. However, when you get stuck in routines, life can end up being lackluster and get predictable and even boring. It is therefore important to step out of your routines every once in a while and get out of your comfort zone. Try to explore other things that challenge you and expand the horizons of your personality. This can help you uncover some talents you didn't know you had.

Letting Go of Guilt

Sometimes guilt is useful, as it links us to our consciousness and prompts us to evaluate our mistakes. Then we can take the right steps towards rectifying any harm we may have caused to ourselves or others. However, too much guilt can be counterproductive to our progress and even detrimental to our personal development. It can keep us stuck in patterns of negative thinking and ruminating about the past. It can prevent us from being able to appreciate the present or be hopeful about the future. If this problem is unresolved, it may lead to negative emotions like depression and anxiety.

If you are grappling with guilt and shame over past mistakes, you need to let go of these in order to become more accepting of yourself. Here are some of the steps that you can take towards this end.

Correct Any Outstanding Wrongs You May Have Made

As we have mentioned, feeling guilty isn't always a negative emotion. It is necessary to accept the consequence of our actions if they have hurt others in a significant way. Feelings of guilt can spur you to right wrongs you may have committed in the past. Therefore, if you feel guilty about a mistake you have made, you can take the initiative to make amends. Granted, it might feel awkward and uncomfortable to reach out to people you have hurt. However, in doing so, you will be able to minimize negative thoughts you may be harboring about whatever happened. Sometimes a genuine apology can be sufficient enough to make amends. It depends on what you feel guilty for doing! If you are not able to directly make amends, think about donating time to an organization that helps others. Do good deeds.

Challenge Your Hindsight Bias

Sometimes we tend to overthink our past mistakes because we validate our hindsight bias too much. It is easy to look back at your past mistakes and make idealizations about how you could have handled the situation better. The truth of the matter, however, is that it is not always possible to predict the outcome of a situation when making decisions in the moment. Even well-meaning intentions can lead to undesirable results. Therefore, when working out your guilt, it is important to challenge your hindsight bias and acknowledge situations where you were acting with noble interests even if the outcome was not what you hoped for.

Challenge the Belief of Over-Responsibility

There are times when we struggle with guilt due to an inflated sense of responsibility. We may wrongly assume that we are responsible for things that happen even when they have absolutely nothing to do with us. If you tend to hold yourself accountable for things that you are not responsible for, you are setting yourself up for stress and misery. It is therefore important to realize that some things are not in your control and you shouldn't hold yourself accountable for them. This will help you overcome the tendency of guilt-tripping yourself, and allow you to be more accommodating of your limitations.

Learning to Forgive Ourselves

The ability to forgive is universally considered to be one of the best virtues anyone can have. This is because it allows you to let go of any feelings of anger or resentment that you have for someone who has wronged you. Some find it easier to forgive than others. However, while forgiving others is something many people are able to do, self-forgiveness can be harder.

Everyone makes errors at one point or another since no one is perfect. It is therefore important to cultivate the art of forgiving yourself and moving past any mistakes you may have made in the course of your life. Learning how to let go of your past transgressions and moving on will help you safeguard your mental wellbeing and allow you to cultivate self-acceptance.

If you struggle with feelings of guilt and regret, here are some useful tips that can help you become more forgiving towards yourself.

Acknowledge the Mistakes You Made

One of the reasons why we get stuck in patterns of regret and guilt is because we fail to acknowledge the mistakes that happened, and the role we played in the way things worked out. This inability to recognize and acknowledge our past mistakes can hinder our ability to learn from these transgressions and move on from them. In order to forgive yourself and begin healing, therefore, you need to honestly admit to your mistakes and acknowledge how it may have hurt someone or yourself. This allows you to take responsibility for your actions and this will minimize the feelings of guilt that you are experiencing.

Try to Figure Out Your Motivation

In order to forgive yourself for any mistakes you may have committed in the past, it is absolutely vital for you to understand why you behaved in the manner you did. Then you can consider why you feel guilty. For instance, you may have done something that goes against your moral convictions. By finding out why you acted in the way you did, you can more easily forgive yourself for your error. This is because understanding the motivations that led to the mistake will help you avoid repeating it in the future.

Learn to Distinguish Between Guilt and Shame

Feeling guilty when you make a mistake that hurts others is completely normal and can spur you to make necessary changes in your life. However, shame is different from guilt. Feeling guilty is an acknowledgment that you know you did wrong, whereas shame is feeling self-reproach about what happened. You can feel ashamed of your actions or feel ashamed because something happened to you. Both of those situations are different from each other, and different from guilt.

Nobody is perfect and everyone makes mistakes, including the most respected people in society. Shame and remorse are natural emotions that allow you to take responsibility for your guilt and move towards better behavior.

Feeling shame or being ashamed because of something that happened to you is different. You may feel shame because what happened is morally repugnant to you or others. You may feel bad because you feel that you contributed to what happened in some way. You may feel ashamed that you are unable to take action to help yourself move beyond what happened. You are not alone. Talk to someone you trust and don't be afraid to seek professional help to access community resources.

Shame is not a very useful emotion since it only serves to undermine your sense of self-worth. Try to avoid wallowing in feelings of shame and self-blame, since this will only keep you stuck in past mistakes and regrets. This will make it difficult for you to accept and forgive yourself.

Strive to be More Empathetic Towards People You May Have Hurt

One of the biggest hurdles of self-forgiveness is that it requires you to have empathy for those who you may have hurt with your mistakes. To really forgive yourself to have to understand how the person that was hurt feels. This can actually increase our compassion for other people. However, when we are focused on self-forgiveness it may make it difficult to relate to other people since we are focused on ourselves. In order to avoid this pitfall, you need to make a conscious effort to empathize with the people who have been negatively affected by your actions. This way you will be forgiving yourself for how you may have really impacted them, and not for how you think you impacted them.

Make a Conscious Decision to Learn from the Experience

Every human being has at some point done or said something which they are not pleased with or proud of. It is normal to feel guilty when we commit a transgression against others. However, getting stuck in a cycle of self-blame and self-hatred can negatively impact your sense of self-worth. This can make it difficult for you to forgive yourself and move forward. Therefore, when dealing with feelings of guilt over a past mistake, focus on the lessons you can draw from the situation. How would you do it differently next time? No matter how badly you may have messed up, you don't need to beat yourself down forever. Recognize your mistake and view it as a learning experience that will help you make better choices in the future.

Summary

As we come to the end of this chapter, there is no doubt that you have learned many very useful strategies for cultivating self-acceptance. This is very important because it is through self-acceptance that we can get rid of negative thoughts that impact our sense of self-worth. By learning how to practice self-acceptance, therefore, we can get rid of negative thinking and ultimately become more positive individuals.

So, to recap the main takeaways of this very instructive chapter, here are some of the points you need to remember when learning how to cultivate self-acceptance:

- Practice mindfulness and relaxed awareness to bring your feelings and thoughts to the forefront of your consciousness. This will help you foster a deeper awareness of yourself and bring you closer to self-acceptance.
- Cultivate gratitude in your life by appreciating the gifts, talents, and blessings you have. Doing so will allow you to realize your own worth and eliminate the tendency to look down on yourself and the situations you find yourself in. Furthermore, practicing gratitude will help you focus on the positive aspects of your life, and improve your self-confidence and sense of self-worth.
- Learn to be more compassionate towards yourself and avoid the tendency to blame yourself for things you have no control over. Practicing self-compassion will make you more in touch with your inner self and help you navigate the complexities of life in a more positive way.
- Learn to forgive yourself and move past the mistakes of your past. Push away feelings like guilt and self-blame which can be major hurdles in your path to self-acceptance.

Achieving self-acceptance is within your grasp. Make conscious efforts to let go of guilt and show yourself and others compassion.

In the closing chapter of this book, we are going to discuss the concept of radical self-love and how you can employ it to fortify yourself against the problems of negative thinking, overthinking and chronic worrying.

CHAPTER TEN:

Practising Radical Self Love

The art of self-love can be very challenging for people to practice, especially when struggling with the challenges of everyday life. It is easy to forget about our own wellbeing when we are struggling to hold down careers and support our families. However, self-love is a very important element of personal growth and self-acceptance. That is why it is vital to practice the art of loving yourself. Self-love is often misunderstood by people who wrongly assume that self-love means being self-absorbed or narcissistic. On the contrary, self-love aims to get in touch with ourselves, our well-being and our happiness to connect with others. Practicing self-love can be very beneficial to ourselves and the people who we interact with (Stenvinkel, 2018).

By practicing self-love, you can challenge the limiting beliefs you may have about yourself, and motivate yourself to work towards your life's goals. The art of self-love also enables you to develop a greater understanding of your strengths as well as your weaknesses. By cultivating a deep love for yourself, you will be less inclined to overlook or gloss over your shortcomings. Instead, you will recognize that you have flaws just like everyone else. Use that knowledge to make yourself a better person.

You should keep in mind that self-love is not a state of mind to be achieved. As a matter of fact, self-love is a process that requires diligence and constant practice. Our self-love grows gradually the more we continue performing acts of kindness, appreciation, and compassion towards ourselves and others.

Here are some of the powerful ways in which you can foster deep self-love for yourself.

Be Someone Who Loves

It can be very challenging to cultivate self-love if you are dealing with thoughts and emotions that are focused on self-criticism and self-blame. When your self-esteem takes a beating from all the challenges you encounter in life, you may even wonder, "What is there to love about me?" The truth of the matter, however, is that everyone, including yourself, has some positive attributes which other people admire.

Instead of trying to love yourself without conviction, you need to first learn how to be someone who loves. Try to focus on what you love about the people you meet, and most importantly, pay attention to the things you love about the ordinary experiences of life. This can include walking to your office on a nice day or having a conversation with a random stranger. Offer loving statements to those that are close to you. By tuning your body and mind to positive emotions, you will begin to find a lot of things to love in your life. This will allow you to be more open to love, and you will be more likely to receive it.

Tap into What it Feels and Looks Like to be Loved

Being loving toward yourself can be easy when things are going well in life. However, when things aren't working out as expected, it is easy to be self-critical. You may get so caught up in your negative thinking that you forget to be compassionate towards yourself.

The truth of the matter, however, is that it is during such times that you need to show yourself the most love. When you are caught up in moments of struggle, you need to think about what someone who loves you intensely would do or say. Chances are, they wouldn't judge you harshly or look down on you. Instead, they would shower you with love, understanding, and compassion. Contemplating your situation in this way will help you get rid of the tendency to self-blame and berate yourself when you are facing a challenging situation. As a result, you will be able to show yourself more kindness and love.

Don't Compare Yourself

As humans, we tend to compare ourselves to those around us in an attempt to gauge how well or poorly we are fairing, or how good or bad we are. Despite the fact that this tendency to compare ourselves to others is natural, doing so can be very negative in a number of ways. Here are some of the ways in which comparing yourself with others negatively affects your life.

- It makes you presume the worst about yourself.
- It robs you of precious time, which you would otherwise be using to do productive things.
- It prevents you from appreciating your own unique talents and gifts.
- It robs you of passion and the drive to pursue your interests and goals.
- It causes you to resent others.
- It robs you of joy and makes it difficult to find fulfillment in life.

As you can see, there is plenty to lose from engaging in constant comparison to others. Therefore, you should endeavor to quit the habit and begin to appreciate the wonderful things you have in life. Here are some of the tips that can help you overcome the tendency to compare yourself to others.

- Become aware of the detrimental effects that these comparisons have on your self-esteem.
- Start acknowledging your personal successes.
- Learn to appreciate the contributions and successes of others instead of being envious of them.

- Learn to be grateful for your uniqueness as well as the innate talents and gifts that you possess.
- Always remember that no one is perfect and that everyone has their own flaws and shortcomings.

Ask Your Support System for Help

Many times when we are dealing with difficult thoughts and feelings, we isolate ourselves from the people who are close to us. We may feel like we are burdening them with our problems when they already have their own to deal with. However, this only serves to alienate us from the people who care about us. Cultivating a strong support system, on the other hand, can help us push through with our goals and navigate stressful situations much more comfortably. People who have strong support systems generally experience higher levels of wellbeing than their counterparts who lack this resource. Furthermore, they are better able to cope with crisis situations in their lives.

A healthy support system can come from close family members, friends, good neighbors, and even pets. It can also come from support groups and mental health professionals. Some of the ways in which support can be provided are in the form of mental, emotional and financial assistance.

Here are some of the things that you should consider when considering the support system in your life:

- How does talking to them make you feel?
- Do they validate your feelings and emotions?
- Do they give advice that is supportive of your wellbeing?
- Do they tell you the truth even if it is difficult to accept?
- Are they happy for you when you triumph?
- Do they motivate you to be a better person?

By asking yourself these questions about the people in your life, you will be able to identify individuals who are supportive of you. This doesn't mean you should write off those who are seemingly less supportive. It only means that you are more likely to gain positive outcomes from spending time with supportive people when you are in need. Know who they are.

Take Concrete Steps to Create Your Desired Life

There are times in life when you come to the realization that the life which you are living is not exactly the one you want. The necessity of changing your life arises out of the desire to align your life with your personal goals and aspirations. It is important to realize that you are fully responsible for creating your desired life and no one else can help you in this regard. So, if you have determined that the life you are living now does not satisfy your desires, you need to take concrete steps to create the life you want for yourself. Here are some of the main techniques that will help you create the positive and fulfilling life that you dream about.

Decide the Kind of Life You Want

The first step is to figure out what you need to change in your life. This doesn't mean you should overhaul everything. Regardless of how you feel about your current life, there are certain aspects of it that are actually good and do not need to be changed. For instance, you may be satisfied by the relationships and friendships that you have, and hence, there is no reason to change them unless you want to "restart your life". Instead, you need to focus on the things that are less appealing to you. For instance, if you are not happy about your current job, evaluate whether you can change it for one that aligns with your goals and desires for personal fulfillment.

Envision Your Desired Life How You Want it To Be

When you begin to envision your life being the way you desire it to be, you will find that things start to fall into place. Having this mindset will act as a motivator for you to make choices that align with your desired life. You must know what you are striving for in order to consciously work towards attaining it.

Do the Things in Life that Make you Happy

When you are trying to create your desired life, you should think about the experiences that make you happy. This includes your work, hobbies, interests, and relationships. Once you have figured out the things that make you content in life, adjust your behavior such that you experience these with more frequency. Doing so will enable you to develop positive habits and give you control over your negative thoughts.

Create and Focus on Your Goals

To create the life that you dream of, you need to be very goal-oriented. This is the time for you to set your goals, and put in the needed work to achieve them. So for example, if you are trying to get into a certain career, work hard to develop the required skills and academic credentials you need.

Don't Worry About What Other People Think

Although it might sound selfish, creating the life that you desire requires you to focus on yourself and ignore what other people may think about you. While everyone is entitled to an opinion, making your decisions based on other people's opinions is setting yourself up for a life of misery. As long as you are not hurting others, do not worry if they approve of the steps you take to improve your life.

Let Go of Fear

Most people neglect to pursue their goals and create the life they want due to fear of the unknown, and fear of failure. The fear of making mistakes and failing is something everyone has experienced at one point or another. Fear of failure is a natural emotion. However, you need to overcome this fear if you are going to make decisions that steer you towards the life you want to create for yourself. Do not worry about not succeeding. Just try to accomplish your objective. If you fail, you can always try again. As long as your heart is in the right place, nothing should discourage you from chasing your dreams.

Surround Yourself with People You Feel Good With

In order to cultivate self-love, it is very important to spend time with people you feel good around. This is because your interactions with people greatly affect your sense of self-worth and confidence. Spending time with people who motivate and encourage you can help you become more accepting of yourself while also challenging you to become a better person. On the other hand, interacting with negative people is likely to make you more pessimistic and negative about yourself. Therefore, you should strive to spend more time with positive people that help you to learn and grow as an individual.

Cultivate Healthy Habits

An essential part of self-love involves taking care of your physical, mental and emotional wellbeing. Therefore, you need to cultivate habits that contribute to positive outcomes in all areas of your life. This includes eating healthy food, exercising to keep your body fit and taking care of your emotional and mental wellbeing. Stop the tendency to do things simply because you "must" or "should" do them. Instead, only do things that empower you and make you feel good about yourself.

*Be Compassionate When Sh*t Happens*

It is very easy for us to beat ourselves down with negative thoughts when unpleasant things happen, or we make mistakes. However, when we experience failure or disappointment, we need to take advantage of this time to shower ourselves with love. Instead of blaming and criticizing yourself when things don't go your way, endeavor to show yourself kindness and compassion. Learn to forgive yourself when you make mistakes and appreciate the good things that you have accomplished. This will help you overcome the feeling of guilt.

Accept What You Cannot Love

Granted, it can be very difficult to love things that seem to go against your personal values and beliefs. However, this does not mean you should simply ignore them or write them off. On the contrary, you need to focus on appreciating them, because doing so allows you to recognize your own uniqueness as a person. This can give you a greater understanding of your own individuality and enable you to be more accepting and loving of yourself.

Have a "Worry-free" Month

One of the most powerful strategies that can help you develop greater self-love is to postpone your worries in favor of positivity. Create a "worry-free" month where you focus on the good things in your life rather than all of the negative worrisome thoughts that serve no purpose other than to drain your energy. By taking some time to enjoy your life without worry, you can increase your energy and develop the clarity of mind and perspective that will help you face your worries when you really need to.

Summary

This final chapter has focussed on fostering self-love and compassion for ourselves. You will no doubt agree that self-love is very desirable. Practicing self-love can significantly help reduce your tendency to ruminate over negative thoughts which erode your personal sense of self-worth. By cultivating self-love, you can overcome the tendency to worry and overthink (Stenvinkel, 2018). Here are the main points you need to remember when trying to cultivate radical self-love:

- Try to focus on the things you love about your everyday experiences, no matter how trivial they may seem.
- Stop the habit of comparing yourself to others and realize that you are a unique individual in your own right. Develop an appreciation for your inherent talents, skills, and gifts.
- Identify your support system and develop a deeper connection with them.
- Clarify your vision of your desired life, and make the necessary changes to live in a way that is more aligned with your vision.

- Spend more time interacting with people who motivate and challenge you to become the best version of yourself.
- Cultivate healthy habits that promote your physical, mental and emotional wellbeing.
- Learn to love yourself even when things do not work out according to your plans and wishes.
- Develop an appreciation for the things which you cannot love and learn to accept them instead of avoiding them.

The practice of self-love will provide you with a deeper understanding and appreciation of your individuality. This can empower you to strive towards your goals and create the life you desire.

FINAL WORDS

As we come to conclude this book, I am confident that the wisdom contained herein provides a clear pathway to eliminating the problem of negative thinking. This problem, as we have learned, is a natural phenomenon that we have inherited as humans over the course of our evolutionary development. It arose out of our need to survive, and provide us with the ability to identify factors that threaten our survival, thereby allowing us to tackle these issues. However, while negative thinking is a natural habit that helps us adapt to our environment, problems arise when we overthink and dwell on negativity. This often interferes with our ability to function and affects our mental and emotional states.

In this book, you have learned techniques to help you clear your mind of negative thinking. You have learned why it is important to identify the source of your negative thinking. By analyzing various cognitive distortions, you can overcome them by ascertaining the validity of your negative thoughts. You also learned about the very effective technique of "name it to tame it" and how you can use this strategy to dissociate yourself from your negative thinking patterns. This will allow you to view them from an objective perspective and reduce their negative impact on your internal state.

Furthermore, we debunked the common misconception about overthinking, which is the belief that overthinking is a permanent problem that cannot be solved. In our exploration of this subject, you have seen how the problem of overthinking arises and the various strategies that can be employed to overcome it. These strategies include reconnecting with the immediate world around you, replacing negative thoughts with positive ones and cultivating a psychological distance between yourself and your negative thoughts. This will help to open your mind to more positivity.

Finally, you learned three main ways you can eliminate your negative thinking patterns forever: cultivate positive thinking, foster self-acceptance, and practice self-love. You now realize the importance of letting go of guilt and forgiving yourself, and how this can help you become more accepting of yourself as a unique individual in the world. We also discussed the concept of radical self-love and how it can help you foster a deeper understanding and appreciation of yourself as an individual. Some of the ways to cultivate self-love include stopping the comparison of yourself to others, becoming goal-oriented, surrounding yourself with positive-minded people and practicing healthy habits in order to safeguard your overall health and wellness. By practicing radical self-love, you can change your overall outlook on life and approach it from a perspective of optimism and confidence. Self-love will also enable you to develop a high sense of self-worth and enhance your self-esteem. When you eliminate negative thinking, you can use the new positivity in your life to create the life you dream of.

I would like to express my confidence in the fact that this book meticulously illustrates the problem of negative thinking and provides brilliant yet simple ways to overcome negative thoughts and worries. All of the strategies and techniques outlined herein have been proven to be very powerful and effective when it comes to overcoming negative thinking. The simple nature of these strategies means that you can implement them in your own life very easily. Negative thinking, although faced by everyone, manifests differently in each individual because we have unique experiences. Therefore, it is ultimately your responsibility to determine how best to practice the techniques we have discussed throughout the course of this book. If you feel like you need additional help or support to deal with your negative thoughts, don't hesitate to reach out to professionals who can guide you.

During the course of this book, I have endeavored to cover this subject matter as comprehensively as possible. However, this is not to say that this book is a conclusive manual on everything regarding the subject of negative thinking. Although you will find the wisdom contained herein very practical and applicable in your real-life, there are also plenty of other resources, both online and offline, that can help you build more knowledge about this subject matter. Take the initiative to explore the subject widely if you want to take what you have learned here to the next level.

In conclusion, what I would like you to take from this book is that negative thinking is not a life sentence. As difficult as it may be to deal with your negative thoughts sometimes, you can use them to help you develop a better understanding of yourself. Therefore, do not feel hopeless or doomed when you experience these uncomfortable negative thoughts. Instead, consider them a challenge to be overcome and a stepping stone towards greater personal growth. With this mindset, you will find it easy to eliminate negative thinking, take control over your thoughts, and shift your focus into positive thinking, self-acceptance and radical self-love.

RESOURCES

Bloom, S. (2015, July 19). 7 Ways to Clear Your Mind of Negative Thoughts. Retrieved February 12, 2020, from https://www.pickthebrain.com/blog/7-ways-clear-mind-negative-thoughts/

Elmer, J. (2019, July 19). 5 Ways to Stop Spiraling Negative Thoughts from Taking Control. Retrieved February 11, 2020, from https://www.healthline.com/health/mental-health/stop-automatic-negative-thoughts#5

F, L. (2008, September 10). The Path to Unconditional Self-Acceptance. Retrieved February 11, 2020, from https://www.psychologytoday.com/us/blog/evolution-the-self/200809/the-path-unconditional-self-acceptance

Grohol, J. P. M. (2019, June 24). 15 Common Cognitive Distortions. Retrieved February 11, 2020, from https://psychcentral.com/lib/15-common-cognitive-distortions/

Holland, K. (2019, January 22). Positive Self-Talk: How Talking to Yourself Is a Good Thing. Retrieved February 11, 2020, from https://www.healthline.com/health/positive-self-talk

Hurst, K. (2014, October 3). 7 Steps To Cultivating A Positive Mindset. Retrieved February 11, 2020, from https://www.thelawofattraction.com/7-steps-to-cultivating-a-positive-mindset/

O'Brien, M. (2019a, December 20). The Four Keys to Overcoming Negative Thinking…for Good. Retrieved February 11, 2020, from https://mrsmindfulness.com/the-four-keys-to-overcoming-negative-thinkingfor-good/

O'Brien, M. (2019b, December 20). The Four Keys to Overcoming Negative Thinking…for Good. Retrieved February 11, 2020, from https://mrsmindfulness.com/the-four-keys-to-overcoming-negative-thinkingfor-good/

Oppong, T. (2020, January 3). Psychologists Explain How To Stop Overthinking Everything. Retrieved February 11, 2020, from https://medium.com/kaizen-habits/psychologists-explain-how-to-stop-overthinking-everything-e527962a393

Positive thinking: Stop negative self-talk to reduce stress. (2020a, January 21). Retrieved February 11, 2020, from https://www.mayoclinic.org/healthy-lifestyle/stress-management/in-depth/positive-thinking/art-20043950

Positive thinking: Stop negative self-talk to reduce stress. (2020b, January 21). Retrieved February 11, 2020, from https://www.mayoclinic.org/healthy-lifestyle/stress-management/in-depth/positive-thinking/art-20043950

Raftlova, B. (2019, September 19). 5 Reasons You Should Stop Comparing Yourself to Others. Retrieved February 11, 2020, from https://www.goalcast.com/2017/03/11/reasons-stop-comparing-yourself-others/

Robinson, L. (2020, February 6). How to Stop Worrying. Retrieved February 11, 2020, from https://www.helpguide.org/articles/anxiety/how-to-stop-worrying.htm

Soleil, V. (2019, August 9). 7 Key Benefits of Positive Thinking. Retrieved February 11, 2020, from https://www.learning-mind.com/7-key-benefits-of-positive-thinking/

Stenvinkel, M. (2018, February 22). Be Good to Yourself: 10 Powerful Ways to Practice Self-Love. Retrieved February 11, 2020, from https://tinybuddha.com/blog/be-good-to-yourself-10-powerful-ways-to-practice-self-love/

YOUR FREE GIFT

Thank you again for purchasing this book. As an additional thank you, you will receive an e-book, as a gift, and completely free.

This guide gives you 14 Days of Mindfulness and sets you on a two-week course to staying present and relaxed. Practice each of the daily prompts to learn more about mindfulness, and add it to your daily routine and meditations.

You can get the bonus booklet as follows:

To access the secret download page, open a browser window on your computer or smartphone and enter: **bonus.derickhowell.com**

You will be automatically directed to the download page.

Please note that this bonus booklet may be only available for download for a limited time.

9 781647 800840